How to Run Better Business Meetings

A Reference Guide for Managers

The 3M Meeting Management Team

McGraw-Hill Book Company

New York St. Louis San Francisco Auckland Bogotá
Hamburg Johannesburg London Madrid Mexico
Milan Montreal New Delhi Panama
Paris São Paulo Singapore
Sydney Tokyo Toronto

Library of Congress Cataloging-in-Publication Data

How to run better business meetings.

  Rev. ed. of: How to run better business meetings /
B. Y. Auger. 8th ed. c1979.
  Includes index.
  1. Meetings. 2. Communication in management.
I. Auger, B. Y. (Bert Y.). How to run better business
meetings. II. 3M Meeting Management Team.
HF5718.H69 1987   658.4′563   86-10355
ISBN 0-07-031029-7

  234567890 DOC/DOC 893210987

ISBN 0-07-031029-7

The editors for this book were
R. A. "Dick" Johnson and Lorin Robinson of 3M and
Martha Jewett and Rita Margolies of McGraw-Hill,
the designer was Naomi Auerbach, and the production supervisor
was Teresa F. Leaden. It was set in Baskerville by Braun-Brumfield, Inc.
Printed and bound by R. R. Donnelley & Sons Company.

Contents

Preface

About the 3M Business Meetings Team and This Book

The business meeting today, as it has been for generations, is management's most useful tool for getting its job done.

But today's meeting has been made more important by the constantly increasing flow of information pouring out of computerized information systems. Now, more than ever, the meeting has become the place where data are sorted, analyzed, regrouped, and distributed. As the speed of information dissemination has increased, the ability to handle it has become more vital. There is little point in speeding up the flow of information if the result is an unmanageable glut. So the need for efficient meetings is greater today—and likely to increase in the coming years.

This growing need is the reason for this book. Its sole objective is increasing the efficiency of business meetings ranging from the seemingly routine working meeting to the powerful top-management decision-making conclave.

The book was written by the 3M Business Meetings Team, five of whom are professionals in the Audio Visual Division of the 3M Company whose daily job is to work in the business meeting field. As a matter of routine, this team analyzes, plans, critiques, and considers every aspect of business meetings. In 30 years of work, members of the team have had ample opportunity to learn why some business meetings succeed and others fail. They have been able to study the physical aspects, such as meeting formats, visual techniques, room layouts, and the like. They also have been able to look past these physical aspects into the basic function of the meeting—solid communication that leads to strong results. The combined experience of the members of the team, past and present, is reflected in the following pages.

The atmosphere in which the team has worked was created by a highly successful management philosophy—the hallmark of the 3M Company—which long ago recognized that management is actually the process of steering the energies of people who have innovative ideas. Out of these interactions come management decisions, corporate planning, products, their marketing, etc. It is obvious that the business meeting is a crucial part of this management process.

This book was designed to be a quick and ready reference on all aspects of business meetings, from how to plan, format, and chair them to how to design graphics used at these meetings. It has been arranged so that each subject appears in the index. A quick glance at the headings in the index should lead directly to pertinent information on any aspect of the meeting, with no need to thumb through the book. Mindful that no executive or manager has time to waste when information is needed, the book was designed to provide instant guidance.

The book can also serve as a guide for managers new to the planning and running of business meetings. It provides an insight into even the most elementary parts of the meeting, such as the maximum number of lines that should be placed on a visual, as well as its more complex psychological aspects. If one idea predominates, it is that the dollar cost of business meetings today may well exceed the benefits derived from them, chiefly because not enough attention has been paid to how they should work. Executives and managers aren't too different from carpenters when it comes to tools. The good carpenter knows the right tool for each task, uses each one in the best way, and keeps them all sharp. The poor carpenter struggles along with dull tools and uses whichever tool is at hand even if it is not the best one for the job. Both are likely to finish the job; but the good carpenter does it faster and better, and the completed work reflects the preparation time in terms of lower cost and better work.

At 3M, we have a strong, twofold, vested interest in business meetings. Our first interest stems from our own calendar of meetings. Within 3M, which has 87,000 employees, we hold thousands of meetings each year to make decisions, formulate plans, review programs, and pass along information. Many years ago we became sensitive to the fact that meetings cost money, and that one way to increase management effectiveness, cut costs, and increase profits was to make our meetings more productive. Every hour saved through more efficient meetings was money in the bank.

Our second vested interest in meetings is that for nearly 30 years 3M has marketed meeting tools such as the 3M Overhead Projectors and Transparency Makers. Our sales force learned early that you can't sell business meeting tools unless you can show the customer why they are needed and how to use them. They had to delve deeply into meeting methods and techniques. This led to intensive studies within the company and to commissioned studies by such organizations as the Applied Research Center at the Wharton School, University of Pennsylvania, and the University of Minnesota.

Out of this interest came the 3M Business Meetings Team. Members of the team developed and conducted, and still conduct, seminars and workshops in meeting planning, meeting management, and the design and preparation of visuals.

In 1964, as an outgrowth of our studies, we published the first edition of *How to Run Better Business Meetings*, by B. Y. Auger. The book was an effort to make available in one package all that we had learned about what makes good meetings. During the next 20 years, this book went through eight revised editions, including four in foreign languages, and more than 100,000 copies are still in use.

Today, however, the pace of advancing technology is so rapid, and speed of communication has become so vital that the old text has been put aside and an entirely new book has been produced. This book reflects not only advances in equipment—the computer and its peripherals, for example—but also changing language and learning patterns.

3M isn't the only company to develop an awareness of the importance of business meetings, of course, but we have had meetings under our microscopes for longer than most.

The New Learning Techniques

Whether we realize it or not, we now absorb information in a different way than we did before the advent of television. Prior to 1950, we were programmed from the beginning of our schooling to learn from the printed page. When audiovisual equipment was introduced, this pattern didn't change at first because the visuals were simply used as illustrations of text. Our learning was still rooted in the printed page.

Then came television, which, at first, was static, too. In early TV, the camera often stayed on one speaker or actor for half a minute or longer as he or she delivered the lines. Then it cut to the next speaker and held the picture again. In time, TV directors discovered *pace*. Instead of one picture held for 30 seconds, we began to see multiple "cuts" of the speaker from several cameras. Half a dozen 5-second pictures popped on the screen during this same 30 seconds—close-ups, long shots, shots of the faces of other people. Action, movement, and change became the director's watchword. Pace, once controlled by the plot of the story, now became a function of visuals.

This brought to the audience a sharpened sense of pace, change, and excitement which has carried over into how we learn and how we participate in meetings. We have acquired a new sense of pace and a new appreciation of the value of the picture.

At one time, a teacher wrote lessons on the blackboard, talked through what was written, then erased the board and wrote again. Today, the teacher flips on the overhead projector, slide projector, or the video tape player. The material on the screen is fast, colorful, and dynamic. The pace has become an important part of the learning process.

Because of TV, then, we now tend to learn by this rapid-fire technique. We absorb from pictures rather than text, and we become bored when we see the same picture for too long. This change has affected the dynamics of business meetings and presentations. The meeting of today can't be geared for the older, slower pace. The material presented, and the method of presentation, must be tailored for this new audience. Our 3M Business Meetings Team has experienced this change, and this book reflects what it has learned.

The meeting is management's most important tool of communication. Like the scalpel in the hand of a surgeon, it should be used deftly. When it is, the results are measurable—fewer wasted executive hours, better and faster decisions, more effective communication, and, ultimately, lower cost for better management.

This book is intended for management at all levels of experience. It will be particularly useful to middle and entry-level managers in the early stages of their careers. By mastering the art of conducting meetings, they become more valuable to their companies and, as a corollary, open up greater opportunities for their own advancement. But seasoned veterans of the management arena should review it, too. The technology of the meeting is moving right along, and the techniques junior managers learned on the way up are a little gray around the edges now. A refresher may be in order.

1

The Meeting under a Microscope

The ideal business meeting is an organizational jewel. It proceeds without wasted motion from opening to adjournment. It is well-planned, has a defined purpose, adheres strictly to a prepared agenda, and proceeds crisply, dispatching each item on the agenda. When it is over, everyone can leave the room knowing something has been accomplished.

Good meetings bring forth the best in people—the best ideas, the best decisions, and the best follow-up reactions. Not all meetings are good meetings, but good meetings *can* happen, and when they do, the company and the individual participants reap the benefits.

There is a certain amount of magic when people come together for a meeting. The magic is in the interplay of ideas and personalities that takes place in the meeting room. When the interaction is completed, information has been exchanged, old concepts and ideas have been tested and blended, and new ones have emerged. One of the magical aspects of a meeting is that it can and should be so many things at once— a communication device, a cauldron of creativity in which new ideas are born, and an anvil on which solid plans are forged.

It also can be the greatest waster of time since the legendary water cooler in a turn-of-the-century office.

Definition of a Meeting

A meeting is any kind of purposeful coming together of people to carry out the business of the company. In this book, we are chiefly concerned with formal meetings involving four or more persons—the typical business meeting for communication, planning, setting policy, making decisions, or motivating the sales force. To be effective, these meetings need to be well planned and executed.

Dr. Peter Drucker, in his book, *The Effective Executive*, says "We meet because people holding different jobs have to cooperate to get a specific task done. We meet because the knowledge and experience needed in a specific situation are not available in one head, but have to be pieced together out of the knowledge and experience of several people."

Meetings and the Communications Chain

Today's executives and managers must be professional communicators as well as astute decision makers. No executive sits alone. Each is tied to others in the company and to the rest of the world by an amazingly fast communications network. Technology has speeded the flow of information, and the amount of data available has burgeoned. Executives and managers today have more information at their fingertips than ever before, and have it much faster.

While this vast inflow of information may improve their decision-making abilities, it also puts them in the hot seat. They must analyze and assess the information quickly, then communicate it clearly to others, fielding it the way a major league shortstop handles ground balls. If they can't handle the task, they become weak links in the communications chain. Hence the critical need to be professional communicators.

The meeting is the executive's chief tool for communications, so as the information explosion continues, the meeting assumes greater importance. The faster data come in, the greater is the company's need for meetings.

The Role of the Meeting in Business Communications

The true role of the business meeting as a communications tool may be lost in the endless chain of meetings that executives and managers must attend. Meetings often become "just another meeting," and only occasionally, "a big meeting." Each meeting deals with its own set of problems or decisions, some of them pretty small. The sense that each meeting is a part of the bigger picture—the profitable operation of the company—wanes. "My life," one executive told us, "is a long string of meetings held together by coffee breaks and lunches." Asked if he thought the meetings were important, he said instantly, "Of course they are," and then added thoughtfully, "but sometimes it is hard to remember that."

It is useful to take an overview of the meeting role. Look at a mythical national marketing manager for a moment. He or she receives daily information through a high-speed communications system from offices around the country. This puts him or her on top of sales and marketing trends, and is critical to decisions for the next month, quarter, and year. Decisions arising from this information affect not only sales and marketing, but also manufacturing, finance, planning—every aspect of the company.

The information is digested, then passed to the staff and other managers. As a result of the information, decisions and plans must be made. New products or product changes may be indicated. New offices may need to be opened or old ones relocated. Policy may need to be restated. In short, the rapid inflow of information may demand a series of critical, effective meetings. The meetings must be held promptly to take advantage of the information.

The role of the meeting as an informational interface is obvious. Through good meetings, the company can produce a timely strategy to respond to the changing market and profit from the technology which provided the information so rapidly. If the meetings flounder and the strategy takes months to develop, the marketing window of opportunity is likely to close. The original information might just as well have been delivered by pony express for all the good it does. To this company, the information explosion turns out to be a tiny pop.

One of the major keys to the successful utilization of today's high-speed data flow is the successful meeting—the subject of this book.

Working Meetings

Not all meetings, of course, dramatically affect the lifeblood of a company. Most are working meetings, seemingly ordinary and sometimes humdrum events that result in minor decisions and small steps forward. They don't provide much to be excited about, and if they run long or don't seem to get much done—does it really make a difference?

It does. Any meeting, no matter how insignificant it may appear, that takes 2 hours when it could have been run in 1, or that doesn't accomplish the work on its agenda, sooner or later affects the company's profit picture.

The 3M Business Meetings Team has worked for more than 30 years with companies of all sizes, from entrepreneurial enterprises to multimillion dollar corporations. We have seen that good meetings make a difference. First-hand observation indicates that there is a clear relationship between any company's growth and the effectiveness of its in-company communications. Poor communication results in confusion, slow decisions, poor utilization of management personnel, lagging competitiveness, and wasted money. Effective communication contributes to growth and profitability.

In short, poor meetings cost money. Good meetings add to profits.

Why Do Business People Dislike Meetings?

If meetings are so important, why do business people seem to dislike them? Executives and managers constantly complain that they suffer from "meetingitis." When they write articles about meetings in business magazines, they almost always open by calling them boring, a waste, or a nuisance. Cynicism about meetings is rampant. John Kenneth Galbraith has said that, "Meetings are indispensable when you don't want to do anything." Commenting on meaningless meetings, William A. Nail, Director of Public Relations for Zenith Electronics Corporation, paraphrased Karl Marx with the observation that, "Meetings are the opiate of the executive class."

Dr. Peter Drucker, in his book *The Effective Executive*, reflects, with tongue in cheek, the attitude of many executives and managers when he says, "one either meets or one works. One cannot do both at the same time."

Meetings clearly are management's best and most-used communications tool. Growth and profitability depend on good meetings. An individual's growth within a company is often related to his or her meeting performance. Yet many business people view meetings sourly and call them a waste of time. Why this dichotomy?

After years of observation, we have come to think that meetings are disliked because too many of them are poorly run—and should be disliked. If the majority of meetings were effective, the criticism might disappear. Executives and managers actually enjoy meetings that get things done. They just don't see this kind often enough.

As for work in meetings—in effective meetings the leader *works*, the participants *work,* and the meeting itself is *a working device.* When it is over, progress has been made and things which needed to be done have been done.

Business meetings should be powerful tools deftly wielded by competent, well-trained executives and managers to effectively achieve the aims of the organization.

The Problems with Meetings

The most common criticism of meetings is that there are too many of them, but this isn't the only illness from which they suffer. Here are some others that will be familiar to anyone who has attended meetings for more than a few months:

- Meeting is too long.
- Meeting agenda contains too much.
- Meeting competes with other important meetings.
- Too many people are at the meeting.
- People who should have been there are not.
- People who don't need to be there are and clutter up the dialogue.
- Meeting is poorly planned.
- Meeting is called for insufficient or spurious reasons.
- Meeting is too long because of poor leadership.
- Meeting is allowed to end without concluding the business at hand.
- Attendees are unprepared to participate.

The Source of Poor Meetings

Why are there so many poor meetings? One reason is that many executives and managers have had little opportunity to learn the techniques of planning and staging a good meeting. Schools with business curricula as a rule do not teach young management aspirants how to run a meeting—in spite of the fact that after graduation, these people will spend a considerable percentage of their next 40 years in meetings.

The common method of learning about meetings is on-the-job training. Business organizations assume that young management candidates will learn about meetings simply by participating in them. As Bill Nail at Zenith puts it, "The young manager is expected to learn about meetings by taking part in bad meetings."

"We attend too many meetings without ever seeing the structure of the meeting," Nail says. "It's a forest-and-trees situation. Too often, no thought is given to the method and format of the meeting. We just meet."

Meetings that get nothing done aren't new or recent. The Broadway musical, *1776*, points this out as John Adams sings about the ineffectiveness of the Continental Congress, meeting in Philadelphia to produce the Declaration of Independence:

> *We piddle, twiddle and resolve!*
> *Not one damn'd thing do we solve!*
> *Piddle, twiddle and resolve!*

Every executive and manager probably would have liked to sing that refrain at one time or another.

Many companies, like 3M, recognize the value of properly run meetings. These companies train managers in meeting techniques, have meetings specialists on staff to ensure effective meetings, and constantly monitor meetings, searching for ways to improve them. But for every such company, there are 10 that simply call meetings.

In an earlier edition of this book, Bert Auger, for many years involved in 3M's Audio-Visual Division and now retired, wistfully said, "I have been in the meeting business for a long time. I have seen within our own organization great improvements, but I must say that, on the average today as I tour the world, I still see about the same ratio of bad meetings to good ones . . . (Those companies with bad meetings) still don't realize they have a problem."

Things haven't changed much since Auger said that, except that the pace of doing business has continued to increase and the need for good, effective meetings is greater than ever.

Good, Bad, and Unnecessary Meetings

There are, it seems, three kinds of meetings—good meetings, bad meetings, and unnecessary meetings.

In this book, we will show how to analyze meeting situations to get rid of the gatherings that really aren't necessary. Then we will look at how to turn the bad sessions into good ones.

Every good meeting has certain qualities:

1. It has a purpose all participants know and understand.
2. It has an agenda organized to achieve that purpose.

3. The people invited to the meeting need to be there, either as contributors or to gain something from it.

4. The meeting is briskly chaired, sticks to the agenda, and accomplishes the work goal with no wasted time or motion.

5. Visual presentations are used when possible, and the visuals are clear, sharp, colorful.

6. Participants understand their roles, come prepared, and make contributions.

7. The chair summarizes what has been accomplished.

8. There is an organized postmeeting follow-up.

When one or more of these fundamentals is not present, you have the makings of a bad meeting.

Is This Meeting Necessary?

This is the first question all managers need to ask whenever they get the impulse to call a meeting. Many unnecessary meetings or meetings that would be of poor quality can be eliminated if the question is answered honestly. The full answer can be found by answering a couple of other questions.

1. *What is the purpose of this meeting?*
   Identify a clear purpose right at the start. Adopt an attitude of—no purpose, no meeting. Most managers who take this approach are surprised at the number of meetings they decide not to call because a clear purpose can't be found. A good rule to follow: If you can't write a single sentence stating a precise and limited objective for the meeting, don't call it.

2. *Is this the right time?*
   Are the time and circumstances right? Is the situation ripe for discussion? Is all the information in? If the meeting is premature, you may be forced to call it off halfway through and set another one later on when the information becomes available. Aborted meetings are wasteful.

3. *What will happen if I* don't *call a meeting?*
   This is a critical question. If the answer is, "Nothing," then there is no reason for a meeting. The meeting would be held simply for the sake of meeting. But if it is determined that without the meeting a decision will be delayed or that vital information won't get to those who need it, there is a good reason for the meeting.

4. *What alternatives do I have?*
   Sometimes a meeting is the best way to go. Often, however, a series of phone calls or a memo can serve the same purpose at much less cost.

5. *How much will this meeting cost?*
   Are the expected benefits of the meeting worthy of the investment? This is the standard return-on-investment question that all managers must answer for every contemplated project. Cost is the unanswered question in most business meetings. It is easy to call a meeting, and the cost is hard to pinpoint because no dollars change hands or appear in the departmental budget. But every meeting costs money and the manager has the responsibility for seeing that the company gets its money's worth in meetings as well as in the other items in the departmental budget.

Reasons to Call a Meeting

There are many good reasons to call a meeting, just as there are many good reasons to refrain from doing so. Most of the legitimate reasons, along with some rationale for each, can be found in the following list.

1. *To accept reports from participants.* Two good reasons for a report meeting are the opportunity to clarify the report with good graphics and exhibits, giving it life and making it memorable, and the possibility of stimulating discussion that can lead to good follow-up action.

However, long reports can produce long, dull meetings. When a report threatens to weigh too heavily on a meeting, distribute it to participants for review several days before the meeting to lighten the burden. The meeting can then consist of a visual presentation or brief summary of the report's high points, followed by discussion.

Whenever possible, replace dull report reading with a well-paced presentation which employs visuals that get to the heart of the report. But allow time for preparation of the presentation. A poor presentation can destroy an otherwise incisive report.

2. *To reach a group judgment or decision.* This meeting provides each participant with an opportunity to express opinions or beliefs which temper the final decision. A consensus grows from this input. It is important for these meetings to arrive at a "voted" consensus. Often, meeting leaders simply sense the feelings of the participants and adjourn the meeting without a final statement of the findings. The good meeting leader brings every participant down on one side or the other of

the question, establishes a clear majority, and sums up the meeting by saying, "It is the consensus of this group that . . . . "

Participants need to know from the opening of the meeting that they are expected to arrive at a decision. A sense of responsibility is an important aspect of the decision-making meeting.

Executives and managers should avoid the mistake of calling a decision-making meeting if the decision has already been made in their own minds. Participants soon recognize that they have been convened for a less-than-honest reason. If only a review or approval of an already-made decision is wanted, the group should be told in advance that the meeting is "for review and approval."

3. *To analyze or solve a problem.* When a problem has been identified, group discussion brings insights and experience to bear on it. A solution or an acceptable course of action should come out of the meeting discussion. To be effective, this type of meeting must have a well-balanced interplay of ideas, experiences, facts, contradictions, and insights. The leader should serve as the moderator of the discussion without trying to sway the group or impose opinions on the participants. The best results come through interaction.

In some instances, these meetings can pinpoint a problem when only symptoms are known. If sales have sagged on the west coast, for example, the meeting task may be to work from the symptom to the problem and then address the problem itself.

4. *To gain acceptability for an idea, program, or decision.* Everything needs to be sold at sometime to someone, and new ideas, new programs, and even decisions are no exception. One good test of new ideas and programs is how well they are received in a meeting. If they don't stir enthusiasm, it may be that they don't deserve it.

In addition to selling the idea, the meeting leader usually wants active support for a proposal or decision. A proposal that doesn't have enthusiastic backing may be headed for trouble.

It is axiomatic that those who contribute to making a decision are the ones who do the most toward carrying it out. In any meeting called to gain acceptance of a proposal, the group should feel that the proposal can be modified and that its contributions are welcome. The group's support is more easily won when the program isn't stuffed down its throats.

5. *To achieve a training objective.* Every meeting is a training ground for its participants. In meetings, younger managers can observe the techniques used by the company's more seasoned executives to arrive at decisions, solve problems, and convey information. While meeting

attendance should always be kept to a practical minimum, thought should be given to the training of tomorrow's executives.

6. *To reconcile conflicting views.* Sharp differences of opinion are common and useful in business. The interplay of opinions is a creative, dynamic force. But if disparate viewpoints develop and are left untended, they can broaden into warfare within the office. Meetings at which both sides can air their views help to keep the questions open and developing. Once positions have been taken on a proposition, backing away can be difficult. Sometimes a graceful, face-saving escape hatch is needed. This can be provided at a meeting attended by the contending factions along with other participants who do not espouse either side. If the meeting is skillfully planned and carefully chaired, the contenders can find room for movement.

7. *To communicate essential information to the group.* This is one of the most necessary of meetings. Its effectiveness often depends heavily on good visuals and a communicator who can breathe life into dull statistics, explain their nuances, and offer explanations to clarify them. Information that might be open to broad interpretation—or misinterpretation—should always be presented in a meeting rather than by memo. The presenter can answer any questions and steer the group away from misinterpretation. The use of the modern tools of meetings such as visuals and displays helps to make the material clear and meaningful.

8. *To relieve tension or insecurity by providing information and management's viewpoint.* Meetings can be effective antidotes for rumors. They are the best way to explain and interpret bad news, which, if left unattended, can career out of control. A meeting for these purposes allows the attendees to hear the news from an authentic, trustworthy source, and gives them a sense of being on the "inside." This is a lot better than hearing the news in the rumor mill, where it is sure to be expanded, distorted, and misinterpreted.

9. *To ensure that everyone has the same understanding of information.* The art of communication is at best imperfect. Twenty people can read a memo and each arrive at a somewhat different understanding of what was intended. Meetings minimize the risk of misunderstanding when information is complex. The meeting group can ask questions until a good understanding is reached.

10. *To obtain quick reactions.* How will people react to a decision? To a new program? A new policy? How bad is a problem? How good is the solution? Managers formulating decisions, programs, and policies some-

times worry that what they propose may be badly received. One way to test the waters is through a small meeting. The agenda should make it clear that the purpose of the meeting is to get individual reactions.

The problem with meetings of this type is that indecisive executives and managers may use them as crutches. Being unsure, they call a meeting as a security blanket for every decision. This is one source of unnecessary meetings and participants quickly recognize them as such.

Use these meetings with care. Make positive presentations and specifically ask for reactions, not approval. Listen to the reactions and make adjustments if they seem necessary.

11. *To reactivate a stalled project.* Administrative log jams are a common problem. They usually are caused by a lack of an individual decision somewhere in the organization. One method to force the decision is to call a meeting to put the topic to a discussion. Often filled with political ramifications, this is a difficult type of meeting which should be used sparingly.

12. *To demonstrate a product or system.* The "show and tell" meeting to announce new products or systems can be minor or major, depending on the need. Internally, it can be used to familiarize employees with the company's new products and generate a feeling of "we are all in this together," and to announce and explain such things as new policies or benefit programs. Externally, it is the most effective way to show new products to dealers, distributors, the press, and the public. These meetings tend to be costly, but have a clear payback. They require careful long-range planning.

13. *To generate new ideas or concepts.* When new ideas or concepts are needed, call a creative meeting. These are quite different from the regular working meeting. In effect, they are unstructured intellectual free-for-alls. The participants are asked to address a problem and let their ideas run free—contributing whatever comes into their minds. Brainstorming is a common technique in advertising agencies, often used in company advertising, public relations, and sales promotion departments, and sometimes used by engineers, product developers, and researchers. Creative meetings are frequently used for naming a new product, developing advertising concepts, or building promotional campaigns.

There is only one ground rule in a good creative meeting: no idea, regardless of how strange it sounds, is criticized, rejected, or laughed at. Once the participants have thrown aside their normal inhibitions, a creative meeting is fun and ideas flow like water. A list is kept of all ideas presented, and later those that look most profitable are selected and explored. The winnowing process continues until a few fully developed ideas survive for final evaluation.

There are other reasons to call meetings, but this list covers most. The important common denominator in the list is that each situation *requires* group action or participation. If this common denominator can't be found, then the meeting probably shouldn't be called and alternate means of communication should be investigated.

Staff and committee meetings and meetings of company groups below the management level—such as Quality Circle meetings—are special and are covered in later chapters.

Meetings Cost Money

When the annual sales meeting or a spectacular event to announce a new product line is staged, the cost is known and budgeted. Costs of travel, hotel rooms, meeting rooms, banquets, and entertainment are estimated in advance and justified. Management reviews these costs and concludes that, given the desired result, such meetings are cost-effective.

But for every spectacular event, there are hundreds of other meetings in the company for which cost-effectiveness is never measured. Yet every meeting must pay its own way. It should have a definite purpose, clearly laid out beforehand, so that the results can be evaluated for cost-effectiveness. There must be a return on the investment.

Often, meetings accomplish less than they should, take more time than they should, involve more people than they should. As a result, they are not cost-effective. If several 2-hour meetings are needed to do what should have been done in a single 1½ hour meeting, then the company is paying too much for the benefits derived from the meetings.

According to a number of surveys, executives spend 40 percent or more of their time in meetings, and, by their own admission, feel that much of this time is wasted. Can this waste be translated into actual dollars? If it can, the executive or manager has a useful guide to help in determining whether to call a meeting.

How to Determine the Cost of a Meeting

Most managers are shocked to discover just how much meetings actually cost. We have developed a simple rule of thumb to estimate the per hour cost of a meeting:

Double the value of the base pay of each participant.

If five people meet for an hour, and each makes $40,000 per year, their salaries for that hour total $96. Salary, however, is only a part of the story. To it must be added payroll taxes, fringe benefits, and general overhead. Consideration must be given to secretarial and preparation time. By doubling the base pay of the participants, these expenses are roughly accounted for.

Doubling the hourly salary figure in the meeting of five persons making $40,000 a year brings the total cost for the meeting to $192. To this figure, add any special preparatory expenditures such as photocopying, slide or transparency, and printing costs.

Table 1.1 can serve as a ready computer for calculating meeting costs. The salary figures shown are already doubled. To use the table, just add up the salary figures for all of the persons present. The total will be the per hour cost of the meeting.

If four persons in the $30,000 bracket meet for 1 hour, the cost to the company is $115. When the meeting extends to 2 hours, the cost is $230. If a company averages ten 2-hour meetings like this each week, the real dollar cost is $119,600 per year—a figure that doesn't appear in any budget. If by good meeting management, the number of sessions can be cut in half, the company saves nearly $60,000 a year.

This savings will not appear directly in the bottom line, of course. It will show up as increased productivity—more and better work for the same dollars. It will show up, also, as expanded work capability for each meeting attendee. By controlling meeting costs, a company could experience strong growth or expansion without adding new managers because the present managers would be able to handle additional responsibilities.

A Budget for Meetings

From time to time, we have thought about creating a departmental budget item called "Meetings." Every manager would be required to anticipate in his or her budget the annual number of meetings of four or more people for the department. During the year, the cost of each meeting would be reported as a departmental expense item. Such budgeting would accomplish several things. First, managers would begin to take a hard look at every meeting. The accountability factor would enter the game and for the first time, the cost of meetings would become important. Second, management would find itself confronted with two figures it has seldom seen: (1) the actual number of meetings held each

Table 1.1 Cost of Meetings to Nearest Dollar per Hour

Annual salary	Number of participants									
	10	9	8	7	6	5	4	3	2	1
$50,000	$481	$433	$385	$337	$288	$240	$192	$144	$ 96	$ 48
$40,000	$385	$346	$308	$269	$231	$192	$154	$115	$ 77	$ 38
$30,000	$288	$260	$231	$202	$173	$144	$115	$ 87	$ 57	$ 28
$25,000	$240	$216	$192	$168	$144	$120	$ 96	$ 72	$ 48	$ 24
$20,000	$192	$173	$154	$135	$115	$ 96	$ 77	$ 58	$ 38	$ 19

year in the company and (2) the actual annual cost of meetings to the company.

The system would demonstrate that there is no such thing as a free meeting. A good management could apply the same cost-cutting techniques to meetings that it does to other expense items, and the eventual result would be leaner, more effective, less costly management.

Alternatives to Meetings

A hammer is an effective tool, but if the need is to saw off a section of 2 by 4, a hammer isn't much good. There are times when a meeting is exactly the right tool to get a management job done. There also are times when a meeting is the wrong tool. The meeting may be too costly or too cumbersome for the task. Or perhaps there isn't time to properly prepare for a meeting. Then an alternative tool is needed.

Four alternatives are readily available.

1. Personal executive action.
2. Written communication—usually the memo.
3. Individual telephone conversations.
4. Conference telephone calls.

It is wise to consider all of these possibilities before calling a meeting.

Personal Executive Action

The quickest, most effective method for most run-of-the-mill decisions is personal executive action, perhaps backed by one or two advisory chats—either by phone or face-to-face across a desk. If the decision involves new policy or procedure, is complex, and requires the input of considerable information, or will have far-reaching effects, then a meeting should be called.

The Memo

The memo as an alternative to a meeting has some advantages. All recipients receive the same information, which can be reviewed several times by each person if necessary. Persons up and down the line of command, some of whom might not be called to the meeting, can be informed. And finally, the memo can be filed as a permanent record.

Memos, of course, have limitations. The writer may not get his or her thoughts down clearly and the readers may misinterpret them. The writer may be too brief and fail to communicate—or may err in the other direction and dictate four single-spaced pages that no executive wants to take the time to read.

The language and style of the memo should be straightforward. Its objective is not to impress people with the writer's ability to create magnificent prose. Its only function is to convey information briefly and clearly. No one has yet offered a Pulitzer Prize for the most creative memo.

The Telephone

No person in business has to be sold on the value of the telephone. Obviously, a phone conversation is a type of meeting, and a few well-placed phone calls often can provide all the information and advice needed to make a sound decision. The phone is a logical candidate as the best alternative to a meeting. Telephone meetings, however, can be as ineffective as any other. To make them work, preparation is needed. They can't just be run off the cuff. Later chapters on how to prepare for a meeting apply also to telephone meetings.

The conference call has become popular because it adds a more interactive dimension to the telephone, making it possible to have phone meetings involving more than two persons. It also can be restrictive in that discussion is somewhat curtailed. Each person must carefully wait a turn to speak. Most useful of all is the speaker phone, which allows a meeting with several participants in each office.

Conferences employing television, telephone, and computer technology take advantage of important new meeting techniques. Electronically equipped meeting rooms bring together executives in widely separated locations in face-to-face meetings. Anyone speaking in these meetings may be seen all along the network. Graphics such as the artwork for a proposed ad can be put on the screen for everyone to see, revisions can be made right on the screen, and a consensus reached almost instantly. In most of these systems, hard copies of graphics and text can be transmitted quickly to each group by facsimile machine or computer.

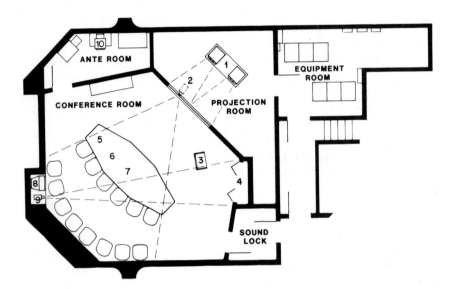

Figure 1.1   The 3M Video Conferencing Facility is typical of the electronic meeting rooms now in operation. It has a (1) rear-screen video projection system to display simultaneously conferees at distant locations and color graphics; front (2) and overhead (7) cameras to picture meeting members and items on the table; a room monitor (5) to show the image being sent to distant points; a podium (3) with two built-in TV monitors to show the presenter both incoming and outgoing video; a panel (6) for control of all room features; a lecture monitor (8) that allows presenters at the podium to see distant conferees; (9) a camera that transmits images of presenters, items displayed on the dry marker board (4) and objects placed in the front of the room; (10) slide/film chain, ¾-inch video player/recorder, photocopying machines, fax machine. Not shown are a videotape player, a 35-mm slide projector, an Encrypton Controller which allows transmitted signals to be encoded, and strategically placed room microphones.

Video teleconferencing is already in use on an international basis, and variations of the technique will play a major role in business meetings of the future. Some systems are complex and require a technician to operate the control panels at each meeting room. Simpler systems don't offer as many advantages but can be operated by the meeting group without help.

Electronic conferences need even tighter planning, better graphics, and better presentations than in-person meetings. Because the hourly expense is high, time must be used very effectively. But when these meetings are well-run, the payback in saved executive time and travel expense makes them very cost-effective.

Summary

The ideal business meeting proceeds without wasted motion from opening to adjournment. It has a defined purpose, adheres strictly to a prepared agenda, and crisply dispatches each item on the agenda. The good meeting brings forth the best ideas, the best decisions, and the best follow-up reactions.

Every good meeting has certain fundamental qualities:

1. A purpose all participants understand.
2. An agenda organized to achieve that purpose.
3. People at the meeting who need to be there.
4. An agenda that is adhered to.
5. Visual presentations used when possible.
6. Prepared participants who make contributions.
7. A summary by the chair of what has been accomplished.
8. An organized postmeeting follow-up.

When one or more of these fundamentals is not present, you have the makings of a bad meeting.

The first question to ask before calling a meeting is, "Is this meeting necessary?" Examine each opportunity to call a meeting by asking these questions:

1. What is the purpose of the meeting?
2. Is this the right time?
3. Do I have alternatives to a meeting?
4. What result do I want from the meeting?
5. What will happen if I don't call the meeting?
6. How much will the meeting cost?

Meetings can be called:

1. To accept reports.
2. To reach a group judgment or decision.
3. To solve a problem.
4. To gain support for a program.
5. To train future managers.
6. To reconcile conflicting views.
7. To communicate information.
8. To relieve tension by providing information.
9. To be sure that everyone understands the information.
10. To get a quick reaction.
11. To reactivate a stalled project.
12. To demonstrate a product or system.
13. To facilitate staff communication.
14. To explore new ideas and concepts.

Meetings are not always the answer. The subject may not require a meeting or a meeting may be too costly or cumbersome. That is the time to consider meeting alternatives:

1. Personal executive action.
2. Written communication.
3. Individual telephone conversations.
4. Conference telephone calls.

Understand the causes of bad meetings so as to avoid them. The things most often wrong with meetings include:

 1. Too many meetings.
 2. Meetings too long.
 3. Meeting agendas contain too much.
 4. Meetings compete with other meetings.
 5. Too many people at meetings.
 6. Wrong people at meetings.
 7. Needed people not at meetings.
 8. Meetings poorly planned.
 9. Meetings called for weak reasons.
10. Poor chairship.
11. Meetings end without a conclusion.
12. Participants unprepared.

2

Your Personal
Stake in
Good Meetings

Meetings are more than just tools of communication. They are training grounds for future executives.

This chapter looks at the meeting as a means of training new executives and as an executive search device for managers. It also looks at them from the personal point of view—as a platform on which future executives and young managers can display their talents. These useful aspects of the meeting are often overlooked but are important to both corporate and personal growth.

E. C. Kilgore, retired Associate Administrator for Management of the National Aeronautics and Space Administration, writing in *Management* magazine, says, "Any organization is only as good as its people; its future is generally only as sound as its ability to select and develop the next generation of managers. Most executives would agree that this premise is at least more true than not. However, in practice, many top executives tend to relegate people development to a lesser priority—to be concerned about only if time allows.

"Even a cursory examination of the best managed and most productive corporations and government agencies reveals a close correlation between success and the priority given to growth and development of managerial talent. It would be an oversimplification to claim this as the sole reason for success; however, it may well be the key to continuing vitality of all organizations."

Meetings to Recruit New Managers and Executives

In our expanding economy, growing corporations are constantly faced with a shortage of managerial talent. Most prefer to develop their own executives and managers and to promote from within, going outside and paying large fees to executive recruiters only when the necessary talent isn't available intramurally.

The scarcity of talent requires every member of management to be on the alert for promising individuals who stand out as "comers" in the company. They need to look for people with ideas, people who demonstrate the capacity to tackle and solve problems, and people who give evidence of being able to direct other people successfully. They must find individuals who show signs that they can run some phase of the business. For some positions, such as sales supervisors and sales managers, marketing executives must look for people who have very specific training and talents in addition to managerial abilities.

Meetings are an ideal activity in which to search out people with these potentials. The meeting offers a unique opportunity to see individuals performing among their colleagues—analyzing situations, presenting ideas, persuading others to points of view and to action. Their knowledge in specific areas quickly becomes evident. The potential sales manager, for instance, who must possess depth of product and marketing knowledge as well as the ability to motivate people, usually demonstrates these capabilities in the span of a few meetings.

Typically, managers evaluate those who work for them through daily observation. They see them in action, working together and interrelating in the same office, exchanging memoranda, creating reports, making recommendations, trouble-shooting, etc. This is an effective method. However, their performance at meetings, either as leaders or as participants, gives an added dimension to the appraisal. No other business activity provides a better insight into the qualities of leadership each staff member possesses.

In the very large organization, with offices scattered around the country, meetings often are just about the only opportunity a manager may get to fully evaluate his or her people, to see them on their feet, communicating, thinking, and reacting. Impressions from meetings, added to an appraisal of the work of individuals in the field, provide a strong feeling for the potential capability of an individual.

The sum of this is: meetings are of great value in evaluating the capabilities of potential managers.

Climbing the Executive Ladder

As a manager takes on more responsibility, moving upward through the organization, he or she attends more meetings, participates in more sessions of critical importance to the company, and meets with more executives at higher levels both inside and outside the company. It is clear that the higher up the executive ladder an individual climbs, the greater the need for an ability to run and participate in meetings. As noted earlier, executives spend 40 percent or more of their time in meetings. Their effectiveness as executives depends heavily on their ability to make the most out of these meetings.

Top management's view of the personnel-evaluation value of a meeting was expressed by Frank Considine, Chief Executive Officer of National Can Corporation, in an article in *Fortune* magazine. He said, "A meeting is really a peer-level review. It's very revealing. You see how someone thinks, how he answers a difficult question, and whether he is an ordinary thinker."

The Meeting to Develop New Managers

In some measure, every meeting has a training value for those who participate. Most of the time, this training is accidental. But many managers use the meeting specifically for personnel development. Some call meetings for the sole purpose of forcing their people to cope with difficult problems—when they themselves already know the probable solution. These meetings have a triple value. They are valuable as teaching tools; they provide the opportunity to see young managers under pressure; and they sometimes produce a better solution than the manager had already envisioned.

One manager of a public relations department with whom we worked makes it a practice to direct his staff to hold two planning sessions each year. The objective of each meeting is to project the activities of the department for the next 6-month period.

"I attend only as an observer," he told us. "They appoint their own leader, prepare their own agenda, design presentations, and produce a report which is given to me. Many fresh ideas have come from these sessions, but the meetings aren't always successful. I can remember two occasions when I cancelled meetings 10 minutes after they began. It was obvious that they had been so poorly prepared that nothing could be expected from them. The cancellations taught the group that good meetings were expected, however, and these days the meetings usually are well done.

"There is a dual purpose for these meetings—the training of my people in running meetings, and the exercising of their creative thinking processes. As future managers, the members of the group need this type of exercise."

There is no better way to bring management talent along than to expose it to the dynamics of group action and reaction—not only in meetings among themselves as just described, but as observers and/or participants in higher-level meetings. People being groomed for higher responsibility can gain deep insights into the management process by observing how their seniors engage in decision-making, problem-solving, and planning.

The role of management is a continuous proposition, and one of its purposes is to provide instruction which will make its members more valuable to themselves and to those for whom they work. Training, too, is a continuing process. One meeting doesn't constitute a graduate course in good meetings. One of the real pleasures an executive or manager can experience is to observe the growth and emergence of younger managerial talent—from a nervous and bumbling first meeting to a smoothly run, effective meeting later on. When the beginning manager begins to exhibit the ability to handle all phases of meetings, he or she usually can be marked for advancement.

Meetings Teach Organization

Two elements basic to all communications, and to meetings in particular, are *organization of thought* and *definition of goals*. Any successful meeting presupposes both well-defined goals and a logical organization of materials to be presented. The meeting shouldn't be overlooked as a tool for teaching these attributes. Because the lessons learned from this work carry over into all of their other business activities, young managers should be given as many hands-on chances as possible to study a meeting subject, define the goals of the meeting, and to organize their thoughts in respect to it.

Understandably, managers prefer not to suffer through badly run meetings, and sometimes only assign meeting responsibilities to experienced people in their departments. But like the basketball coach who must play the first- and second-year students this year if there is to be an experienced senior team 2 years from now, managers have to look ahead. The first-year students must gain experience.

As one manager told us, "I drop my beginners into the deep end of the pool. I assign a meeting to one of them who has never run one before, and allow a couple of weeks for preparation. Then I find out whether he or she can swim. Mostly, they panic the first week, settle down to serious work the second week, and when the time comes, they swim. They don't break records, but they swim."

Bert Auger once described the business meeting as a continuing seminar, an ongoing education on business management. He called it, "one of the best post-graduate courses you can take."

Visual Aids for Training

The creation of visual displays such as slides and overhead transparencies to accompany presentations also is an excellent teaching device. Nothing forces greater concentration on the logical organization of materials, awareness of time, and effective communication. Forced to compress a report or other presentation into a given time period, the presenter must think through the material, analyze it to discover its critical points, and determine the best ways to illustrate those critical points.

Presentations, those involving visuals in particular, are self-testing. The person who created them must stand before the audience and present them. For most, this is an enlightening and educational experience. Audience reaction tells instantly whether their judgment was right or wrong. They tend to learn quickly from a couple of these experiences. It is always interesting to compare an individual's third or fourth presentation to the first one. The improvement usually is enormous.

Specifically, the creation of presentation slides and overhead transparencies trains one because:

1. They force order and sequence in the presenter's thinking.
2. They require selection and itemization of key ideas while guarding against the omission of other vital points.

3. They teach time conservation by keeping the speaker on the track and to the point.

4. They instill confidence in the speaker, lessen self-confusion, and promote the habit of essential thinking.

Penetrating questions during and immediately following the presentation offer an automatic grading device. If the presentation generates a lively discussion without the need of many clarifying answers or explanations, the presenter knows the grade for the effort is an A. On the other hand, if key points were left out or the emphasis was improperly placed—and it is necessary to make further explanations before any discussion can begin, our presenter can move the grade down to B or C.

An Open Letter to Management Trainees

This section is addressed to persons who have just entered the management arena. Look at meetings as a great opportunity. Through them, you can contribute to the company, broaden your own business and management knowledge, and make way for future career advancement. Don't make the mistake of being afraid of meetings or of taking them too lightly. Consider them as what they are—powerful management tools. The sooner you learn to use these tools effectively, the sooner you begin to carry your weight in your organization. One way to use these tools is to be an active, effective participant; another is to run good meetings of your own.

If you analyze meetings carefully, you discover that your attention is needed at a number of different levels. The first level, of course, is the business of the meeting—the problem under discussion. The second level is what others do at the meeting. By watching the more experienced members of the company at work, you can acquire a liberal education in general management techniques. The third level is the specialized knowledge displayed at the meeting. You can deepen your own field of competence quickly by careful observation of what others with your training do. Whether you are in accounting, sales, purchasing, or research, meetings can serve as a postgraduate course in your chosen field.

It isn't easy to split your attention this way during a meeting, but once you are aware of the different levels, it becomes easier. Probably the most beneficial thing that you can do is think about the meeting after it is over. Recall how it was conducted. Mentally review how the business of the meeting was carried forward, what techniques the participants employed to get their ideas out, and what new facets of your own specialty you saw at work. Analyze any mistakes you observed. Why did one member of the group fail to make a point? Would you have tried a different tack? One of the few values in poor or ineffective meetings is what they can teach you. If the meeting wasn't good, what caused the failure? Knowing the answer will some day save you from making the same mistake.

Especially in your early weeks in a new job, meetings teach the functions of the department. You quickly learn where the different responsibilities are lodged—essentially, who's in charge of what. Later, when people from other departments come to your meetings or when you attend interdepartmental meetings, your management education is broadened considerably. You begin to understand how jobs interrelate and how corporate tasks intermesh. You learn to tie together all of the functional aspects of running a business. You learn to see the other person's point of view. More importantly, you learn the overall company point of view. This is all subsequently reflected in your own work. You can gain so much from meetings if you recognize their many significant aspects right from the beginning.

The really satisfying experience comes with the opportunity to run meetings of your own. They may be minor affairs at first, but take them seriously. Recognize that ballplayers learn in the minors, then become stars in the majors. Plan every meeting carefully. Think in terms of a well-defined meeting objective and an agenda designed to achieve that objective. Do your homework and leave as little as possible to chance. The planning and running of a meeting isn't difficult, but it requires work. A meeting cannot be approached in an offhand manner and be successful.

The one other big step is your first full-scale presentation, complete with an array of visuals. When the assignment is first handed out, you will be seized by panic—we've all been through that—and wonder if there isn't some way to plan a business trip for that day, or perhaps develop a welcome case of the flu. The panic will pass in a few minutes, and then you can settle down to intelligent planning. Start by looking at the topic, making a list of the data and information needed for the presentation, and then note after each item where it can be found. It's a good idea to gather all the information quickly; that way, you'll have more time for the organization of the script and the visuals.

The preparation of the script and the visuals is covered in other chapters. Follow the instructions closely, and your presentation will work. When you have made the presentation, you will face a roomful of critics who will review your thinking and help advance it to the next stage of accomplishment. This can be the most educational part of the exercise.

To bolster your spirits as you prepare that first presentation, remember that meetings provide one of the best platforms from which to make supervisors aware of your personal attributes and potentials. This meeting you are preparing to address isn't a problem. It is your chance to shine.

Summary

The sometimes unseen values in meetings are their usefulness in searching for upcoming management talent and as a means of training young managers for the job ahead. For the young manager, the meeting provides not only an opportunity to learn an important management technique and an inside track for learning about the people and business of the company, but it is also a fine personal public relations platform.

The planning of visuals to accompany a presentation is a particularly effective training method because:

1. It forces order and sequence in thinking.

2. It requires selection and itemization of key ideas while guarding against the omission of other vital points.

3. It teaches time conservation by keeping the presentation on the track and to the point.

4. It instills confidence in the preparer, lessens self-confusion, and promotes the habit of essential thinking.

3

Meeting
Dynamics

Andrew Rouse, Chief Executive Officer of INA at the time, confessed in an article in *Fortune*, that he enjoys a well-run meeting. And he thinks that other executives feel the same way. "Obviously," he says, "there are meetings that waste time. But it's a mistake to say that meetings are a waste of time in business. Meetings *are* business."

There is a real desire in the corporate world for good, well-run business meetings. Executives and managers are result oriented and take satisfaction from participating in a successful operation of any kind, including a meeting. Nothing frustrates them more than a lack of results.

The business meeting is a living, dynamic, but fragile entity with a personality of its own. The person who convenes the meeting controls the personality of the meeting and has the responsibility for creating a positive meeting climate. This is achieved in part by calling the meeting for the right reasons, inviting the right participants, and meeting in the right circumstances. The dynamic forces that affect a meeting begin with a pervasive sense of readiness felt by all the participants before the meeting begins.

Readiness Factors

Good preparation is nine-tenths of the formula for a successful meeting, and the full responsibility for meeting readiness falls on the person who calls the meeting.

The major steps for getting ready are:

- Preparing an agenda.
- Notifying all participants in ample time.
- Making sure all who are invited can attend.
- Making sure the facility is ready.
- Allowing time for preparation of visuals.

For an average in-office meeting, most preparations shouldn't take more than 10 or 15 minutes. The agenda can be pencilled on a pad, then typed. A few phone calls can assure that the selected time is right and that everyone can attend. At the same time, attendees can be briefed on the agenda. None of these items is difficult or time-consuming. However, if they aren't done, the meeting may be severely jeopardized.

The notification of participants does more than just determine that they will be present. Psychological readiness is important. Knowing that a meeting is coming, participants mentally prepare for it. Awareness of the meeting may be only in the subconscious, on the back burner, but it is there. The contribution each participant makes may depend on this back-burner preparation—and is a major reason for advance notice of the subject matter.

If time permits—and it should—a written agenda should reach the desk of every participant several days before the meeting.

Meetings fall apart when some of the invited fail to attend, when an expert to present specific information is not there, or when the discussion reveals that the participants haven't had the opportunity to formulate their thoughts.

A visible lack of readiness affects the central purpose of any meeting. It turns off those who did get ready and delays the final resolution of the meeting's business. When some in the group exhibit a lack of preparation, interest sags around the table. Those who came prepared to grapple with the subject matter now feel deflated. They will find it difficult to work up enthusiasm for the additional meeting that now may have to be called.

It is not good to gain a reputation as a sponsor of meetings like this.

The Personality of a Meeting

The personality of every meeting begins to develop in the hours before the meeting starts and takes form rapidly within a few minutes of the opening. This personality has been labeled as the mood, tone, climate, and other things, but regular meeting goers recognize it no matter what name is applied.

The personality can be positive, negative, or neutral. In a neutral meeting, work gets done but little enthusiasm can be developed. In a negative meeting, little work is accomplished. There is a pervasive sense of failure in the room. Meetings with a positive personality, on the other hand, start off on an up beat. There is a "can-do" sense about them. The objective of anyone who calls a meeting should be to create a positive personality.

A number of factors can help to create this personality. The atmosphere of the meeting place is one; the weight of the subject matter is another. The demeanor of the person running the meeting is a major influence. Right along with it is the sense of purpose instilled by the distribution of a no-nonsense agenda and a clear understanding that the meeting will cover the agenda, getting the job done in the shortest possible time.

"The climate or tone of a meeting," says Joseph Callanan in his book, *Communicating*, " is set by both the physical setting and the behavior of the participants. A pleasant setting with comfortable chairs and good lighting and ventilation tends to put people at ease." He adds, "If people are comfortable with each other and with what's expected of them, they will participate more freely and be more productive in meetings. . . . People will not be completely productive if they are worrying about what is expected of them."

Some meetings seem to open as comedy shows and never recover. Some take place under a cloud of probable failure. Some quickly become battlegrounds and scenes of contention. Others are indecisive before they start and seldom improve in the hour that follows. Good meetings feel confident, like winners, from the first word.

The personality of a meeting is fragile and affected by seemingly small occurrences. Things which create a negative personality of a meeting include:

- The chair arrives late.
- The meeting room is not reserved or ready.
- The chair opens the meeting in a jocular manner, like a stand-up comedian, and encourages levity.
- The chairman appears unprepared, or opens with a vague statement such as, "I'm not sure why we're here but. . . . "
- Participants arrive late.
- The meeting is frequently interrupted for telephone messages.
- Participants demonstrate that they aren't ready by fumbling their way through the discussion.

When the personality of the meeting becomes apparent, the participants feel and react to it. They tend to behave as the personality of the meeting dictates. If it opened as a comedy session, the group finds it hard to get serious. If it opened with apologies from the chair and stumbling from the early participants, it will continue as a lame duck. Serious participants become disinterested. If interruptions destroy the atmosphere of the meeting, the focus may be lost because of the long recaps and reviews needed to get the discussion back on track.

Creating a Positive Climate

The responsibility for setting the positive personality or climate of the meeting lies with the convener. To get the meeting off the ground correctly, the chair must be in control from the inception. In addition to early notification of all participants and seeing that the meeting room is ready before anyone arrives, there are some other things the convener can do to help in the formulation of a good meeting personality.

1. If there are any doubts about attendance, check during the hour before the meeting. If late cancellations endanger the effectiveness of the meeting, call it off before anyone has wasted time on it.

2. Get to the meeting place early and spread papers out for work.

3. See that an agenda is at each participant's place.

4. Call the meeting to order at the appointed time, whether the entire group is present or not.

5. Proceed with the meeting as latecomers arrive. Ignore their arrival and keep the business rolling.

6. Give a clear indication that the agenda will be followed and that the meeting will be finished at the specified time.

The atmosphere of the meeting should be pleasant. Jokes are not out of place and, in fact, can be helpful in establishing a good atmosphere, *as long as they are clearly parenthetical and not a part of the meeting*. When jokes and witty remarks become a part of the meeting, its value as a business tool diminishes.

If the arrival of latecomers is allowed to disrupt the flow of business, the chair may have a difficult time in restoring it.

If anyone indicates the feeling that "I don't know why we are here," then plainly, the preparation was less than perfect. If the majority of the group feels the same way, it becomes clear that the meeting should never have been convened. It should be postponed until proper preparation can be done.

Meeting Roles

Everyone at a meeting assumes a role, consciously or unconsciously. The chair, for example, either assumes the role of leadership or sits back and lets the meeting take its own course. Participants can take active roles in the discussion, simply sit as observers, or play a sniping or devil's advocate part. The outcome of the meeting very often is determined by the roles assumed by those in the room.

Anyone attending meetings needs to think carefully about the roles he or she habitually assumes because they can have a lasting effect. Reputations have been made and lost through meeting roles. The chronic objector, the constant nit picker, and the inveterate speech-maker are soon tagged by their fellow managers, and the nonleading leader becomes well-known. In later evaluations for advancement, these roles may come back to haunt. Meetings are a stage on which executives and managers can demonstrate their abilities. The roles they play should reflect positively, not negatively, on these abilities.

The meeting leader has several responsibilities that dictate the role he or she must play. These include control of the meeting without dominating it; the encouragement of discussion to bring out ideas; and steering the meeting so that the agenda is covered within the allocated time.

The meeting participant has the responsibility of contributing to the discussion, playing neither the role of "rubber stamp" nor of persistent objector. Contributions can be both positive and negative. Offering suggestions that build on the idea under discussion is positive. Pointing out problems or shortcomings of the idea is a valuable negative contribution. The role of the devil's advocate, aggressively challenging the idea, is good as long as the rest of the group understands that the role is being played and that the challenges are not made for destructive reasons.

Who Should Attend?

The attendance list for most meetings is almost automatic, dictated by the reason for the meeting and the responsibilities and functions of the people in the company. But in the interest of improving meetings, it probably shouldn't be quite so automatic. Look at the people who at first glance might be logical participants and measure them against the following yardstick.

Do they:

- Have a solid knowledge of the business at hand? Can they make a real contribution?

- Have the power to make a decision or approve any action agreed on in the meeting?
- Have the responsibility for implementing decisions made at the meeting or for carrying the project to the next step?
- Represent a group that will be affected by a decision made at the meeting. If so, they are a strategic link with the responsibility of carrying the result of the meeting back to their group.
- Need to know information to be presented at the meeting?

Add one other consideration: the development of future managers. As has been pointed out, the meeting room can be a most important training ground. One or more of the meeting participants could be selected on this basis.

How Many Should Be Invited?

The right number of participants depends on the kind of meeting. From the standpoint of dynamics, there are two kinds of meetings, the *presentation* and the *working* meeting.

The Presentation

The presentation is one-way communication, much like a stage show, in which information is offered to the audience by the presenter. Its success depends almost entirely on how good the presentation is: its pace, visuals, logical flow, pointed text. If it is dull and slow, everyone goes to sleep. If it is done well, everyone benefits.

Report meetings, new product meetings, and informational meetings typically involve presentations. The attitudes of the participants are set before they enter the room because they know the kind of meeting to expect and come prepared to listen, learn, and absorb. They arrive with their minds in the "receive" mode.

The right number of attendees for a presentation can range from two to infinity and is limited only by the meeting facility. As long as everyone in the room is comfortably seated and able to see and hear the presentation clearly, the number is right.

One psychological factor should be considered. As the number in the audience grows—usually beyond 25 or 30—the sense of intimacy and personal participation is lost. A feeling of distance sets in. In smaller meetings, each member of the audience can be made to feel that the presentation is specifically for him or her. As the size of the meeting grows, this becomes more difficult. The nature of the presentation and the kind of material to be presented should serve as guides in determining the size of the group.

If the meeting, for example, is to present the details of a new medical benefits program to employees, the material could be presented to 500 at one time, or to groups of 25 in different meetings. The smaller meetings will be more personal, and the employees are more likely to recognize and feel the company's attention to their welfare. The large meeting would be very impersonal—simply a recitation of facts everyone should know about the plan—but informative. Whether to hold a large meeting or a series of smaller ones really depends on the feeling the company hopes to generate and a consideration of the time required for the smaller meetings. The facts will be communicated in either case.

The real danger in presentation meetings is the temptation to fill the room because there is space—without regard for the time-wasting potential. The "right" people for any presentation are those who need to be there. Anyone else is a time-wasting dollar drain.

If a question and answer session follows the presentation, the number need not be restricted. But when the meeting consists of a presentation followed by discussion, the number invited to attend should be held down to make a good discussion possible.

Working Meeting

Working meetings are two-way communication. The core of the meeting is discussion, and participants come prepared to be involved. Problem-solving, decision-making, and fact-finding meetings fall into this category.

The success of the working meeting depends on the ability of the chair to generate and steer discussion, and the willingness of the participants to enter into the discussion. The greater the number of participants, the more difficult both of these become.

"For real face-to-face communications," Leslie This says in *The Small Meeting Planner*, "the maximum is reached at 15. Beyond that, no technique (of meeting management) will do the job. Psychological distance sets in . . . the phenomenon of subgroups becomes quite real, and people 'feel' they are apart."

A meeting grows disproportionately more complex as the number of participants grows. The addition of one or two people may double the communication problems.

A management consultant has worked out the mathematics of the complex interrelationships in a meeting group. When a fifth member is added to a group of four, the new member brings 20 new relationships and, in addition, adds nine relationships to each member of the original group. The addition of the fifth person increases the working capacity of the group by 20 percent, but increases the complexity of the meeting by 127 percent.

Experience indicates that the more complex the subject of the meeting, the more intense the discussion will be—and the fewer the number of people who should participate. Conversely, the lower the level of individual discussion, the larger the number of people who can attend the meeting.

Take it as a given that the more participants there are, the longer any meeting will require to accomplish its work.

Attendance Guidelines

When assembling a list of persons to invite to a meeting, use the type of meeting as a guide.

> For presentations—consider everyone who needs to know.
> For decision-making and problem solving, experts recommend five persons or fewer.
> For problem identification meetings, 10 persons or fewer.
> For informational meetings, keep the audience under 30 to maintain good personal contact.
> For training, especially if there is a hands-on phase, 15 persons or fewer.
> Seminars work best with less than 15 participants.
> For committee meetings, the maximum effective number is seven. As the committee grows beyond this number, its work slows markedly.

The chief rule: Never ask anyone to attend who doesn't need to be there, regardless of the type of meeting.

How about Your Boss?

Is it a good idea for bosses and their subordinates to participate in the same meeting as equals around the table? This is an old question with some prickly aspects.

Can subordinates act as equals under these circumstances? Can they, for example, disagree vehemently with their superiors in a discussion? They are always mindful of the boss's reactions and very aware that when the meeting is over, any equality evaporates. To be forceful in such a meeting requires great skill and tact on the part of the subordinate and tolerance on the part of the executive.

Annette Gaul, writing about staff meetings in *Management* magazine, says that the feeling of dread employees sometimes feel about staff meetings can multiply when one is in a meeting with either employers and/or supervisors. The employee has to look good to all of them. "That problem can be solved," she says, "by avoiding too many levels of people at one staff meeting."

Generally, all meetings should be composed of people with approximately equal status. This assures equality of discussion. Subordinates can be brought in to contribute special knowledge or to act as observers, but usually should participate only to a limited degree in the discussion.

In meetings about controversial matters, opposing viewpoints always must be presented, and those representing both sides *must* be invited. It is particularly important that the opposing views be represented by people of equal status.

Departmental Representation

Many meetings involve more than one department. Sometimes active participation by each department is required, and participants qualified to speak for them must be there. At other times, departments may need representation only on an informational basis and their people are there as observers, not participants.

The danger in these meetings is overrepresentation. Department heads sometimes bring a couple of assistants or send several representatives. Participants in these sessions should be qualified in the same way as participants for other meetings. Can they contribute? Do they have a need to know? The number of observers should be limited.

Then there is the question of authority. If the task of the meeting is to make a decision or set up a plan of action, participants should have the authority to agree for their departments. Time is wasted if Engineering's representative leaves the meeting saying, "I'll let my boss know and get back to you."

More than 15 People?

When more than 15 people legitimately should be involved in a meeting, there is a problem of meeting dynamics to be solved. The large meeting will be slow, ponderous, and probably less effective than desired. One way to solve the problem is to divide the agenda, breaking the large meeting into several smaller sessions. The smaller meetings will take less time and be more effective. Later, two people from each group can meet in a kind of summit meeting to bring the agenda together. Another solution is to select a small working group for the meeting, leaving out many who might have a reason to be there—and then have each member of this group hold separate meetings to relay the meeting's findings. These variations have the disadvantage of creating more meetings, but despite this, they can be cost-effective when the number of persons who should attend the original meeting is very large.

When to Meet

Two factors are always at work when deciding when to hold a meeting: the need for timely results and the readiness of the participants.

Many meetings dictate their own timing. A decision may be needed now, not next week. The sales force has to be fired up before the introduction of a new product, not after it has been on the market a month. These factors usually are beyond the control of executives and managers, who must schedule meetings to accommodate them.

But inside of these time-forcing factors are other considerations.

1. Meet when the participants are at their best. Stay away from Monday mornings, Friday afternoons, and the hour after lunch, when everyone may be sleepy. Don't schedule meetings for the last 15 minutes before the office closes.

2. Avoid surprise meetings. Surprise meetings disrupt the planned workday of those commanded to attend and don't allow the participants to prepare mentally. Mental preparation is essential because the attitude each brings to the meeting plays a role in its success.

3. Give everyone time to prepare physically. Notify them of the purpose of the meeting in advance so they can gather needed materials and notes. In the meeting notification, make them aware of the subject matter to be covered, the role each is expected to play, and the length of the meeting.

4. Make certain the people who need to attend will be available. Check for competing meetings and for travel plans before finalizing the schedule.

5. When a presentation is involved, allow time for preparation. The script needs to be written and edited. Visuals must be designed and made. Extended preparation time for visuals is no longer necessary,

since good slides and transparencies can now be produced quickly, but still, the time must be taken into account. The preparation and production of visuals is discussed in a later chapter. A rehearsal should be planned for any major presentation, partly to assure a smooth presentation and partly to find ways to tighten and improve it.

How Long the Meeting?

How long should a meeting be? Just as long as absolutely necessary—and no longer—considering the material to be covered.

When contemplating how long a time period to schedule for a meeting, remember the effective work span of the participants. Psychologists say that the productivity of a group tapers off after about 1½ hours of work. After 2 hours, it falls precipitously. Any single-session meeting should be less than 1½ hours, with the ideal time about an hour. Longer meetings should be broken into two sessions, with a 10- to 15-minute break between sessions.

The length of the break is important. If it is too long, participants become detached from the subject and find it difficult to reengage after the break. If it is too short, they haven't time to be renewed and refreshed. It's a good idea to indicate the planned break time on the agenda so everyone can look forward to it.

The timing of work sessions and breaks is especially important for all-day meetings. Two good work sessions of no more than 1½ hours each, with a coffee break between, is about right for the morning. If presentations drag on too long, the participants' ability to absorb diminishes quickly and meeting effectiveness is lost. In very long discussion meetings, creative contributions by the participants fall off sharply as the session gets into its second hour.

Chronobiologists call that dull, sleepy period right after lunch the *postprandial letdown.* They say it isn't just the result of eating a heavy lunch, but is a natural work break demanded by the body systems, which need to fall back and regroup after a morning's activity. A heavy lunch may deepen the letdown, but even after a light lunch or no lunch at all it will be there. Don't fight nature. Plan the timing of meetings to get past the letdown. The quick, 30-minute lunch between meeting sessions sounds like a good timesaver, but it may not be. The first hour after lunch could be a dud. By reconvening at 1:30 or 2 p.m., after a break for lunch and the inevitable letdown, the participants may produce better results.

Keep the afternoon sessions short to fight boredom. Three short meetings are better than one or two long ones. They pick up the pace of the day while longer sessions make it feel interminable. The quickened pace livens up the participants and increases their contributions.

The Meeting Place

The meeting place itself has a lot to do with the mood and personality of a meeting, often charging it either positively or negatively. More good work is achieved in positive meetings set in a pleasant working atmosphere.

The majority of meetings take place in an office or conference room simply because the space is convenient and available. But managers have discovered that occasionally switching the site to a nearby hotel or restaurant has some advantages. The switch emphasizes the importance of the meeting, and the refreshing change of scenery often encourages better discussion. Time, however, is the villain, since such meetings can take up to three times as long as in-building meetings. The question the manager has to ask is, "Does the beneficial effect of the switch outweigh the loss of time?" Sometimes it does.

The average office or conference room is a good setting because it takes a minimum of preparation and the atmosphere is generally conducive to a positive session.

One doesn't usually think about preparing a standard office for a meeting. People just come in and sit down and the meeting begins. But a little obvious preparation is psychologically sound and helps to set the mood of the meeting. The chairs should be in place, note pads available, and a projector and screen ready if they are to be used. When the participants arrive, they see that planning has been done and feel from the start that the meeting will not be a waste of time.

Office designers have awakened to the idea that visual presentations are now an integral part of small meetings and not reserved just for the meeting spectacular. The average conference room, once just a big room with a long table, is now equipped with overhead and slide projector equipment. Managers should take advantage of this. The study by the Wharton School of the University of Pennsylvania on the effects of overhead visuals on business meetings, which is discussed in Chapter 8, has shown that meeting effectiveness rises rapidly when overhead projectors are used, compared to meetings without visuals. Meetings are shorter, decisions are reached faster, and participants feel that the meetings are more professional.

Breakfast and Lunch Meetings

Breakfast and lunch meetings work well because they save time. Most break into two parts, the meal and the meeting. Some discussion takes place during the meal, but serious work generally gets under way as the dishes are cleared. Then the convener must step in quickly and focus attention on the subject or face the prospect of losing the interest of the assembly.

These meetings start informally and give participants an opportunity to chat about the subject before the serious discussion gets under way. Away from the office, such conversations are open and less inhibited. The atmosphere of a restaurant or dining room is a pleasant change from the office setting, but the noise level and interruptions by the serving staff must be carefully controlled.

Breakfast meetings, especially if small, short, and well-organized, leave the feeling that they haven't interrupted the workday. Lunch meetings are informal, too, but if they extend much past the normal lunch period, may irritate the participants, giving them the feeling that their working day has been invaded. Dinner meetings have fewer advantages. They come at the end of a busy day, when the participants are weary and ready for rest. They work best as the closing event of a meeting, when they offer an opportunity for informal postmeeting discussion among the participants.

Summary

A meeting is a living, dynamic but fragile entity with a personality of its own. The person who calls the meeting controls the personality of the meeting and has the responsibility for creating a positive meeting climate. This is achieved by calling the meeting for the right reasons, inviting the right participants, and meeting in the right circumstances.

Meeting readiness is also the responsibility of the convener. This includes preparation of an agenda, timely notification of participants, readiness of the meeting room, timing of the meeting, and creation of the positive climate.

Things which adversely affect the climate and personality of a meeting include:

- The chair arrives late.
- The meeting room is not ready.
- The chair opens on a comic level and encourages levity.
- The chair appears unprepared.
- Participants arrive late.
- The meeting is interrupted for telephone messages.
- Participants aren't ready for the discussion.

Who should be invited to a meeting?

- Those with knowledge of the agenda subject who can make a real contribution.
- Those with the power to make a decision or approve actions agreed on in the meeting.
- Those who are responsible for implementing decisions made in the meeting.
- Those who represent a group affected by any decision made at the meeting.
- Those who need to know the information to be presented.

The type of meeting can serve as a guide when assembling a list of people to invite to a meeting.

For presentations—consider everyone who needs to know.

For decision-making and problem-solving meetings, five or fewer persons.

For problem identification meetings, 10 persons or fewer.

For informational meetings, keep the group under 30 for good personal contact.

For training, especially if there is a hands-on phase, 15 persons or fewer.

For working seminars, less than 15 participants.

For committee meetings, seven is the maximum effective number.

When scheduling a meeting, set the time to:

1. Meet when the participants are at their best. Avoid Monday mornings, Friday afternoons, the hour after lunch, and the last 15 minutes before the office closes.

2. Avoid surprise meetings. They may cut into valuable scheduled work time.

3. Allow participants time to prepare physically. Notify them of the purpose of the meeting in advance.

4. Make sure everyone in the group will be available at the selected time.

5. Allow sufficient time for the preparation of any presentation to be given at the meeting.

4

Blueprint for a Successful Meeting

George J. Lumsden, former manager of sales training for the Chrysler Corporation and now a management consultant, points out in an article in *Sales and Marketing Management* magazine that, "We don't prepare foods without recipes or build houses without blueprints. Why should we expect meetings to be successful without plans?"

The agenda is the meeting's blueprint.

The agenda is the one absolute requirement for any successful meeting. It may only be a little scribbling on a bit of paper held in the meeting leader's palm—but the agenda is essential to all meetings, whatever the size or purpose. The agenda is to a meeting as a rudder is to a ship—the steering mechanism. Without it, the meeting is in constant danger of veering off course, failing to achieve its goals, and turning into a monumental time waster. If there is one commandment the 3M Business Meetings Team wants to pass along, it is:

Never begin any meeting without a written agenda.

Some executives have told us that they keep meeting agendas in their heads, and don't concern themselves with writing them out. No doubt some people can handle meetings this way some of the time. But there are so many important benefits to be had from a written agenda that we can't imagine why anyone would not use one.

Others have said they see little reason for preparing an agenda for small meetings. Mr. Lumsden says, "There is a great temptation to consider small, informal meetings unworthy of extensive planning. That's a mistake many sales managers make—it's only a small group, it meets regularly, we all know each other, so let's stay friendly and chatty. However friendly and informal a meeting might feel, it should nonetheless accomplish something. Participants should cover all vital topics and do so within an acceptable period of time."

The agenda ensures that all topics will be covered, that the meeting will move along from point to point, and that something will be accomplished.

The Values of an Agenda

The first value of an agenda is that in putting it down on paper, the executive must do at least a minimal amount of thinking about the order of the meeting. As the agenda items are put down, they prioritize themselves and give the meeting a logical organization. It then follows that first things will be discussed first. This eliminates wasted time and helps to produce good results.

The second value of an agenda is its use as a leadership tool. The meeting leader can check off each item as it is completed. If the discussion strays, the leader can point to the agenda and say, "We're getting away from our reason to be here. Let's get back to the agenda." This reference usually restores order to the discussion. If there are objections, the leader can suggest a later meeting to cover any items not on the present agenda.

The third value of an agenda is its usefulness as a guide to participants. When the agenda is distributed a day or more before the meeting, participants have time to get their thoughts in order, gather materials they might need, and be ready to contribute to the success of the meeting. Even if they don't see the agenda until they sit down at the meeting table, the value is still there. The order of topics for discussion is visible at a glance, and they can prepare to join in.

When there is no agenda, the discussion begins randomly or at the direction of the chair and proceeds without a visible target. The participants join in as the leader cues each topic, but they lack a clear sense of orderly progression toward the meeting's goal. While the work may get done, the working time is always lengthened.

The first step in preparing an agenda is to consider the strategy of the meeting to be called.

Planning the Strategy of the Meeting

Every meeting, large or small, simple or complicated, involves strategy of some kind. Many don't view the planning process as a matter of strategy, but it is. There is a goal to be reached, and a plan is needed to facilitate getting to that goal. In its simplest form, the plan may be no more than a logical listing of the items to be discussed, and the only strategy required is to keep the discussion moving. In more complex meetings, where intermediate decisions must be reached or formidable objections overcome, the strategy can be quite involved.

The first steps in planning the format of the meeting and the strategy to be employed take the form of questions to be answered:

1. *Should I call a meeting on this matter?*
   Answer: After careful thought, during which it is determined that no alternatives exist and that a meeting is the most effective method of achieving what is needed, it becomes clear that a meeting should be called.

2. *What is the goal of this meeting?*
   Answer: What, in very specific terms, should be the end result of this meeting? The question probably was answered as it was determined that a meeting was necessary. However, the answer isn't final until it is possible to write a single sentence in which the goal of the meeting is stated. That sentence becomes the opening statement of the meeting agenda.

3. *What must take place to make the achievement of this goal possible?*
   Answer: In most cases, to achieve any goal—make a decision or determine an action—information must be passed or exchanged, an understanding of the problem must be reached by all participants, and perhaps several smaller decisions arrived at before the final decision can be made. This means a certain number of logical steps must lead up to the final decision. These individual steps should be reflected in the agenda as separate discussion topics.

4. *Who can help to achieve this goal, and who might be a block in the road?*
   Answer: Certain persons can provide needed information. Others have decision-making powers or responsibilities. Some need to be involved for political reasons. Some are known to be chronic objectors. Some are positive thinkers. From this mixed list, those who need be there for reasons of information and/or position on the organization chart must be selected. The need for strategy

becomes apparent if some of those who must be invited are known to oppose the matter up for discussion—or if some on the list *always* oppose any forward movement.

These questions produce three vital pieces of information: What the meeting must accomplish; what information must be presented to make this possible; and who should attend the meeting. These are the skeleton of the agenda.

Assume for a moment that this meeting is called to determine the final retail price of a new product about to be launched. The leader knows the goal and must first decide what information needs to be reviewed and understood to make the decision possible. Perhaps the following information might be needed:

1. Price of competitive products.
2. Marketing position of the new product in relation to competitors.
3. Cost factors of the new product.
4. Forecast of volume and its effect on cost.
5. Advantages and disadvantages of different price levels.
6. Marketing strategies as they relate to cost.

With this information, the participants should be able to make the decision. In rough drafting an agenda, the leader schedules as many short, informative presentations as are needed, and makes a note of the appropriate people to give each report. Much of this information may already be known or have been touched on at earlier sessions, so the leader must determine whether to include quick capsule reviews. To be sure everyone is up to date, such reviews make sense.

Time is allowed for these presentations as the meeting plan is drawn up. A question-and-answer period should follow each presentation for purposes of clarification. The discussion should begin after the presentations. With these reports sketched in, the agenda begins to take shape. The meeting has a goal and a clear set of steps to arrive at that goal.

Guidelines for an Effective Agenda

The agenda is a skeletal outline of the proposed meeting. It can start with a one-sentence statement of the purpose of the meeting, followed by brief topic statements that will guide the discussion. Guidelines for an effective agenda include:

1. The agenda should concentrate on a few major points or issues.

These should be related. If a number of unrelated issues must be dealt with, schedule fewer topics and think about two meetings instead of one.

2. The agenda should be well organized but should not feel so tight that it precludes full participation by everyone in the group.

3. The agenda should be distributed in advance. Two days usually are adequate. For an elaborate meeting requiring serious preparation, particularly of presentations, a week or more should be allowed.

4. The agenda should indicate who will attend, along with an indication of the time and place.

5. The agenda should be an upbeat document. It should reflect opportunities, not problems. If the meeting is called to solve a bad problem—a disaster with no obvious solution—there is little point in burdening the participants with a sense of doom and gloom before the meeting begins. They are being presented with the opportunity to solve the problem, no matter how bad it is, and that should be their attitude as they approach the meeting place.

6. No agenda should open in a negative vein with statements like, "This is the third meeting on this subject after two meetings with poor results." Avoid any statement that automatically classifies the meeting as mundane or routine, such as opening the agenda—or the leader's opening remarks—with "As usual, we will . . . "

7. The agenda should be specific about time. It should indicate the starting time and also the time allocated for each presentation, for discussion, and for breaks. It is probably most important to show the time when the meeting will end.

Setting Up Topics for Discussion

The process of breaking the subject of the meeting into its component parts is the preparation step most in need of attention—and the one that often gets the least. The way these parts are defined can seriously affect the management of the meeting. The components, listed in order and numbered, become the topics on the agenda and actually set the pattern for the work of the meeting.

Each component or topic should be as narrow as possible in definition so as to confine the discussion and prevent rambling. A big umbrella statement like "company sales results" offers the participants very little direction. On the agenda, such a statement needs to be narrowed to a more specific topic such as "rising sales in the first quarter," or better yet, "causes for rising sales in the first quarter." Now narrowly defined, it focuses the discussion and keeps the meeting on track.

Avoiding Umbrella Topics

Generalized umbrella topics lead to generalized discussion. The more specific the topics listed on the agenda, the better control the meeting leader has over the meeting.

In a meeting called to determine next year's marketing strategy for a product, an umbrella topic might be, "Discuss marketing strategy." This is a wide-open invitation to any and all discussion, none of it directed. By breaking this umbrella topic into logical segments, the leader can control the discussion:

1. Review of this year's marketing strategy. Presentation. 5 minutes.
2. Results of this year's strategy. Presentation. 5 minutes.
3. Overview of possible strategies. Presentation. 10 minutes.
4. Discussion of new strategies.
5. Decision on strategy.
6. Summary.

This meeting would start with two quick presentations to review background aspects of the problem, followed by a presentation outlining possible new strategies. These set the stage for a discussion of this year's marketing strategy. Such quick presentations can be great time savers. Without them, several participants are sure to do their own off-the-cuff reviews that take more time and are less comprehensive. Because the scheduled presentations have been limited to 5 or 10 minutes each, participants know that time won't be wasted.

The third item on this agenda summarizes possible strategies. These probably were proposed or discussed in previous meetings. Some undoubtedly already have supporters ready to speak in favor of them—and take up valuable meeting time. By having them reviewed in a presentation format, the meeting leader cuts time-wasting individual reviews and prepares the meeting for serious discussion.

When the third presentation has been finished, the meeting is only 20 minutes old. No time has been wasted. The leader can now say, "Mr. Stanley has outlined some of the possible strategies. If there are any new ideas, let's discuss them now. Then we can get into the process of deciding which is best."

Because of the way the agenda was laid out, the meeting leader has positive control and the meeting proceeds in logical, orderly fashion. Without the agenda to keep order, the first participant to speak might propose a marketing strategy and two or three others might follow with their ideas. Others would jump in with variations. The discussion would be diluted by questions, and it would range widely without a sense of being targeted. Any new ideas might well be lost in the melee. At some point, the meeting leader would have to salvage the discussion, reminding the participants of the final goal.

The well-structured agenda generally avoids the need for such a salvaging operation. It gives all participants the necessary background and presents the likely alternatives. The discussion can then proceed to weigh them, compromises can be made, and a final decision can be reached with a minimum of floundering.

Barriers that Might Arise

A major strategy a meeting leader should consider as the agenda takes shape is how to handle the barriers or roadblocks that might spring up to prevent reaching the meeting goal. Most often, the barriers come from the people who attend the meeting, but the leader can't avoid these problems by being selective. All key people who relate to the topic under discussion must be invited, even though some may be negative or hard to handle. Faced with a mixed group, the leader needs to understand these people and how they work, and anticipate any barriers they might throw up.

Good discussion and the airing of conflicting views are important to any meeting, and the resolution of conflict seldom is easy. But conflicting views must be anticipated, heard, and resolved through discussion so that a consensus can be reached. During the planning stage, the leader's question is: What dissent or conflict can I expect, and how can I steer the meeting through it?

Guiding a discussion through the rough waters of conflict is largely a matter of knowing the positions, temperaments, and personalities of those who attend. Any group has an assortment of personalities—the incisive thinker, the chronic objector, the dissembling speechmaker, the ultraconservative, the bet-a-million risk taker, the nit picker, the shoot-from-the-hip decision maker who acts now and thinks later, the cautious thinker who must mull everything over at length, and the commonsense thinker who cuts through smoke without difficulty. Somehow, all of these must be allowed to express themselves, and then be brought to the point of decision.

The reputations of the participants usually precede them, enabling the leader to plan a meeting strategy. This would include compromises, accommodations, and trade-offs that might be offered to move the meeting around roadblocks; firm meeting discipline to overcome speechmakers and nit pickers; tact for handling the too cautious and the incautious; and firm, logical thinking to keep the discussion flowing. An understanding of how the decisions made at the meeting will affect each person is a help in determining the kind of trade-off necessary to move each participant to a common track that leads to the decision.

Predicting the behavior of meeting participants involves:

1. Knowing the position each is likely to take relative to the subject at hand.

2. Knowing how the personal goals of each individual enter into their attitudes.

3. Knowing their track records in past meetings.

4. Becoming acquainted with personality conflicts within the group which might be expected to surface in an intense discussion.

The experienced executive or manager knows the people in his or her company, so an analysis of the participants usually takes very little time and requires only the working out of the strategies necessary to keep the meeting moving as individual idiosyncrasies come to the surface. But the strategies *must* be worked out or the meeting may get out of hand before the final decision is reached.

In planning the strategy and constructing the agenda of a meeting, a leader often walks a tightrope. Control and discipline are essential, yet too much control can stifle discussion and interfere with the work of the group. Too little control allows the discussion to ramble, with the same result. In addition, the leader must act as an impartial coordinator and discussion leader and avoid imposing personal views on the other participants. The meeting group should be allowed to digest the question and arrive at an opinion of its own.

The Strategy of Assigned Meeting Roles

Earlier we discussed the fact that everyone attending a meeting assumes a role of some type, and that people often become known, for better or for worse, by the roles they assume. Another kind of meeting role is the one assigned by the meeting convener. In planning the strategy of a meeting, the convener often must call on one or more of the participants to do a specific job.

The most obvious role is that of acting as a presenter of information. The convener assigns the task of summing up a body of information to one or more of the participants, and the presentation of that information becomes a part of the agenda. Less obvious are roles assigned to participants in the discussion part of the meeting. In talking over meeting details beforehand, the convener might say, "When we get to item four on the agenda, I'd like you to bring up the question of . . . . " This is one way to be sure that all aspects of a subject are discussed. It is a particularly good way of introducing controversial items into the meeting without putting them on the agenda. It is also a method by which the convener can be sure that all sides of a problem or all viewpoints are represented in the discussion without the need for introducing them from the chair—which may give them unnecessary importance or flag the convener as being on one side of a controversy when he or she should be perceived as neutral.

Inviting Agenda Topics

A good management technique is to invite meeting participants to suggest items for the agenda. In checking with participants on the timing of the meeting and whether they can attend, a leader should outline the purpose of the meeting and the topics to appear on the agenda—and then ask for suggestions. This gives those who attend an immediate sense of participation and of having a personal stake. It is also a good way to find out in advance where some of the roadblocks or opposition may come from. It also serves the leader as a useful backstop, helping to prevent the omission of important points that need to be discussed.

The Agenda as a Disciplinary Agent

The two greatest benefits of a prepared agenda are (1) the way in which it superimposes a logical flow on meeting discussion and (2) its ability to rescue a discussion which gets out of hand.

Anyone who has ever chaired a meeting knows the feeling: what started off as a simple discussion suddenly takes off in an unplanned direction as extraneous ideas and comments are introduced. In 5 minutes, what had been a carefully planned meeting turns into a debating society on subjects which have little relation to the purpose of the meeting. The meeting leader must quickly break up this discussion and get the meeting back on track. This isn't always easy.

The prepared agenda provides a simple, effective method. The leader simply stops all discussion and says, "We are on agenda item four. Let's get back to it." Those participants caught up in the discussion which veered from the agenda quickly recognize what happened and get back to business. If an item of importance came up in the wandering discussion, the leader can restore order by saying, "You are right. That item must be dealt with. But it isn't on our agenda today. We can handle it at another meeting. Now, back to item four. . . . "

Meeting leadership of this type signals everyone that this is a no-nonsense meeting which will get its business accomplished in good time. It is really appreciated by busy people who must spend a lot of time in meetings. The leader who can handle meetings this way quickly gains a reputation as an effective executive.

Multiple-Topic Agendas

Ideally, meetings should be held to a single major topic whenever possible. Single-topic meetings tend to be shorter and have more concentrated, insightful discussion. Short agendas encourage discussion in depth, while longer agendas produce abbreviated discussion. Participants, looking balefully at a long agenda and thinking of the ticking clock, may back away from presenting ideas or engaging in pointed discussion. The long agenda sometimes encourages the feeling of, "Oh, let's get on with this. We have a lot to do."

However, single-topic meetings aren't always possible. Regular staff meetings, for example, almost always consider a collection of topics. The problem then becomes one of organizing the topics on the agenda to keep the meeting efficient.

In organizing a multitopic meeting, first list the topics that must be covered. Review this list to be absolutely certain that these topics *must* be dealt with. The question to be answered is, "Do we really have to take this item up now?" The objective is to limit the meeting to those topics which are essential, timely, and needful of the group's attention. Look to see if some of the topics can't be handled by an alternative method: the memo or the phone call. Is group discussion essential?

Next, organize the topics to produce a logical order. Keep related topics together on the agenda so the discussion can flow from one to the next with a minimum of overlap and repeat discussion. It is sometimes difficult to switch the minds of participants from one topic to the next, especially if the discussion has been lively and imaginative.

With the topics in line, look for evidence of the umbrella syndrome. Is each topic broken into specific agenda items to facilitate discussion? Are some too general to promote good discussion? It is always better to have two or three specific agenda topics than one umbrella topic, because of the meeting control and logical flow the specific topics provide.

Finally, when the agenda appears to be complete, survey it for time. How long will the meeting take? If it looks like it will run more than 1½ hours, two possibilities exist: make it a two-part meeting with a break at the halfway mark, or divide the agenda into two separate meetings. Any two-part meeting will use up the better part of a morning or an afternoon. Such meetings should be reserved for extremely important matters, and never used for a collection of smaller items. It is always more difficult to get attendance at longer meetings because most executives and managers have difficulty in finding a whole morning or afternoon to contribute—unless the subject is crucial. Nothing gives participants a greater sense of "time-wasting meetings" than a long session devoted to relatively inconsequential subjects.

Agendas for Staff Meetings

Staff meetings, by their very nature, are different from other meetings. They need the backbone of a planned agenda to keep them from degenerating into yack sessions, yet they also need to allow freedom of expression. Andrew Grove, author of *High Output Management*, in a *Fortune* article, says that the staff meeting "should be more of a controlled situation than a free-for-all. The agenda should be issued far enough in advance so that subordinates will have prepared their thoughts for the meeting. But the proceedings should also include an 'open session'—a designated time for the staff to bring up anything it wants. This is when various housekeeping matters can be disposed of, as well as when important issues can be given a tentative first look."

Using the Agenda to Get Ready

We have looked at the preparation of the agenda and its several roles during a meeting. It also is a useful checklist for the leader to use in setting the meeting plan in motion. Certain steps must be taken to assure a good meeting and as each is completed, it can be checked on the agenda sheet. The agenda serves as a reminder that:

1. All participants must be contacted. Can they make the meeting? Does the time or place have to be changed to get the right attendance?

2. Presenters must be given their assignments. The leader needs to learn how much preparation time is needed for the presentations and the type of equipment (overhead projector, 35-mm slide projector, etc.) the presenter expects to use. The meeting date may need to be adjusted to allow necessary preparation time, or the meeting room may have to be changed to assure that the proper equipment is available.

3. Participants should be asked for suggestions for topics or subtopics to be included in the agenda.

4. Special speakers or presenters should be contacted well ahead of time—so that alternates can be found if they are not available.

5. Special exhibits or props need to be ordered in ample time.

6. The right meeting space should be reserved for the date and time of the meeting.

7. Arrangements for coffee or other refreshments must be made.

The majority of meetings are relatively simple and require a minimum of make-ready. But even for the smallest, simplest of meetings, readiness must be assured—or the meeting should be postponed until everyone can be ready. Half-ready meetings rank high among the time-wasters. Participants invariably leave them feeling irritated and unfulfilled. They face the prospect of a second meeting to make up for the deficiencies of this one—and they don't like it.

An executive's secretary can take care of checking the availability of the meeting room, making arrangements for refreshments, and typing and distributing the agenda. In some cases, the secretary can poll the participants as to their availability for the meeting. However, a call from the convener is better because it permits a quick discussion of the agenda and preparation time—and lends both a sense of participation and of importance to the meeting.

Using Prepared Checklists

At 3M, we have introduced three preprinted checklists to aid in planning a meeting, notifying participants, and in preparing a short "action-plan" set of minutes at the conclusion of the meeting. Those involved in meetings keep master copies of these checklists in their files and use them to make as many copies as needed when planning a meeting. These forms are illustrated in this chapter.

The Meeting Planning Checklist

The meeting planning checklist (Figure 4.1) reminds the planner to reserve the meeting room, send out the meeting notice, order materials

MEETING PLANNING CHECK LIST

Meeting objective:_____

_____

Participants_____

_____

_____

_____

_____

_____

_____

_____

_____

_____

_____

Date_____

Time_____ to _____am/pm

Place_____

_____

____ Room reserved

____ Agenda (meeting notice)

____ Prepared

____ Sent

____ Visuals prepared

Meeting Materials

____ Note pads, pencils   ____ Name/place cards   ____ Name badges

____ Handouts_____

_____

_____

_____

Equipment

____ Overhead projector . ____ Spare lamp

____ Slide projector . . . . ____ Spare lamp

____ 16 mm . . . . ____ Spare lamp

____ Screen (Size)_____

____ Charts   ____ Pointer

____ Chalkboard   ____ Chalk

____ Video tape/disc

____ Marking pens

____ Microphone

____ Lectern

____ Extension cord

____ _____

____ _____

Food, Beverage

____ Coffee ____ Juice ____ Soft drinks

____ Lunch _____

Post Meeting

____ Action minutes

____ Next meeting _____

Room Layout

Note: Designate No Smoking Area

Figure 4.1   Meeting planning checklist.

such as pencils, name badges, etc., reserve any needed equipment, and gather a list of participants.

The Meeting Notification Form

The meeting notification form (Figure 4.2) is a memo on which the date, place, and starting and ending time of the meeting are entered, along with an agenda, a statement of the meeting's objective, and any premeeting preparation expected of the memo recipient. One of these is sent to each participant.

The Meeting Action Plan

The meeting action plan (Figure 4.3) was designed to replace meeting minutes, yet still provide the essential documentation every participant should receive. Someone at the meeting is asked to serve as meeting recorder and to take charge of this form. As decisions are reached or assignments are made during the meeting, the recorder enters these in the appropriate places on the form. Those attending the meeting are listed on the reverse side. At the end of the meeting, the recorder turns the form over to the meeting leader who has two uses for it. It can go into the tickler file to serve as a reminder of the action assignments for follow-up to ascertain that they have been carried out; and it can be duplicated and sent to the participants as action minutes.

The forms, we find, work very well. The meeting action plan is especially effective in assessing how good the meeting was. Later on a quick perusal tells the leader who was there; whether the meeting started on time, stayed on schedule, and ended on time; whether the agenda items were covered; if the meeting objective was reached; what the work assignments were and whether they were completed.

Following Up the Invitation

Plans change. Time evaporates. Fires flare. The wise meeting convener follows up on meeting plans to be sure that things are moving along without any hitches. A simple meeting without presentations for tomorrow can be called today without the need for follow-up. But if the meeting is set for later in the week or next week, then follow-up is essential. The convener should know that those who said they would attend can still do so, that the preparation of presentations is progressing properly, and that the presenters will be ready.

To:_____

From:_____

Date:_____

MEETING NOTIFICATION

Date:_____

Time: Start:_____   End:_____

Location:_____

Agenda

_____   _____   _____

_____   _____   _____

_____   _____   _____

_____   _____   _____

_____   _____   _____

_____   _____   _____

_____   _____   _____

Meeting objective:_____

_____

_____

_____

_____

Pre-meeting preparation:_____

_____

_____

_____

_____

_____

Figure 4.2   Meeting notification.

_____ Meeting

Meeting date:_____ Recorder:_____

MEETING ACTION PLAN

Chair:_____

Action to be taken	Person responsible	Deadline	Completed

Key issues or discussion

List of attendees attached   Time: End: _____

                                                                  Start: _____

Next meeting:_____ Length: _____

Figure 4.3   Meeting action plan.

When a meeting is scheduled for a week or more away, business occurrences may require an adjustment in the agenda. A topic might have to be added, or the basic purpose of the meeting might need adjustment. A fast phone call or memo to all participants is necessary when this happens. It is seldom a good idea to spring surprises on meeting participants.

The Agenda Should End on a Positive Note

One way to eliminate the negative feelings often associated with meetings is to be sure they end up on an upbeat note. The participants should leave with the good feeling that they have accomplished what they set out to do. Edward F. Konczal, an AT&T staff manager, in an article in *Supervisory Management*, advises meeting leaders to "try to arrange the agenda to end with a positive item—something that is likely to have general approval."

The Power of a Good Summary

The last item on any agenda should be the summary. Meetings should never be allowed to just taper off and, like old generals, fade away. They should be brought to a conclusion by a statement from the meeting leader that summarizes what has taken place, what decisions were made, and what action should follow the meeting. If work assignments for individuals resulted, these should be specified in the summary. If another meeting at a later date was agreed upon, this, too, should be specified. The summary should be concluded by an adjournment statement by the leader.

There is real power in a good meeting summary. Psychologically, it sends participants away with a strong sense of having done their work—and no feeling of having wasted valuable time. Those with specific assignments know what they have to do and when it must be done. In the case of decision-making meetings, the actual decision that was arrived at is stated so that everyone knows and understands it. More than a few decision meetings break up with participants asking each other just exactly what it was the group decided to do.

If there are any doubts about the details of the decision or action resolved in the meeting, they appear quickly after a good summary. Those not sure of the details of the action or who thought a different position was taken, can ask questions immediately and the position can be clarified before anyone leaves the room. All too often, in a meeting requiring a consensus, the leader doesn't summarize, then later reports on "the consensus" as he or she felt it—frequently to the surprise of some of those who were there and remember a somewhat different result.

The summary may be the most important task of the meeting leader. It must be brief, concise, and all-encompassing. Participants must feel that it reflects what actually happened. It cannot be an expression of what the meeting leader hoped would happen but didn't. In some cases, what happened may not be to the leader's liking. The meeting may not have gone the way it was planned. But that shouldn't influence the summary statement. "Sour grapes" statements by the meeting leader in the summary are in poor taste. The tone of the summary should be one of solidarity and cooperation. It should reflect the fact that the wisdom of the group was called upon and went to work.

The Agenda—Once the Meeting Is Over

An agenda is extremely useful in preparing the postmeeting follow-up. By making brief notes on the agenda sheet as the meeting progresses, the leader has a concise set of minutes which can serve as the basis of the brief summary which should be sent to all participants. The 3M Meeting Action Plan form, mentioned earlier, is an excellent substitute for minutes—or can serve as a guide and reminder if the leader chooses to dictate minutes for distribution.

This summary is an important but often-neglected duty. Participants can have short and/or inexact memories in spite of a good oral closing summary by the chair. The postmeeting memo reminds them of what happened and provides an official record of the meeting. As Andrew Grove says in his *Fortune* article, "The chairman must nail down exactly what happened by sending out minutes that summarize the discussion that occurred, the decision made, and the actions taken. It's very important that attendees get the minutes quickly, before they forget what happened." They need positive feedback so they can see the results of the time they spent in the meeting.

Summary

Every meeting, like every ship, needs a steering mechanism. That mechanism is the agenda. The agenda forces logical organization of the meeting, serves the meeting leader as a guidance and disciplinary tool, and tells those who will participate how to prepare.

The steps in preparing an agenda are:

1. Determine the ultimate goal of the meeting.
2. Determine the intermediate steps needed to get to that goal.
3. Select the people who should attend.
4. Consider the possible barriers and ways to get around or through them.

Of these, the second step is perhaps the least understood. In it, the generalized topics in the agenda are broken down into specific discussion items to promote logical meeting thought and provide the meeting leader with better control of this flow. The use of big umbrellalike subjects promotes rambling, time-wasting discussion.

When possible, meetings should be devoted to a single topic. When multiple-topic meetings are necessary, the topics should be organized so that related subjects are discussed in order. Very important topics should be eliminated from multiple-topic meetings and held for separate meetings of their own, in the interest of time conservation and preservation of their importance.

The chair must orally summarize at the end of every meeting to be sure that everyone present has the same idea of what occurred. Once the meeting is over, the leader needs to distribute abbreviated minutes, prepared from notes kept on the agenda sheet or Meeting Action Plan form, to confirm actions and decisions of the meeting.

5

The Meeting Room—
Battle Arena
or Workshop

Good generals survey the battle site before committing troops to an engagement. They learn the advantages and disadvantages of the terrain and determine how negative features can be turned into positives and how the site can be used to give their army the advantage. Students of the battle of the Little Big Horn believe that General George Custer may have rushed his Seventh Cavalry into the battle without looking over the terrain—with disastrous results.

A business meeting is not usually compared to a full-scale battle, but the selection of the site can be just as important to the meeting's outcome as the survey of a battlefield. An inappropriate or ill-equipped site can result in a poor meeting. A well-chosen site sometimes can transform an otherwise weak meeting into something at least passable.

Meeting Atmosphere

"There is almost universal agreement that the physical environment has a significant effect on the psychological environment," says Joseph Callanan, in his book, *Communicating*. "Formal settings induce formality. This may be appropriate for the announcement of an important decision, the signing of a contract, or the promotion of a top executive. But formal settings are not conducive to getting down to real detail work, where you can push chairs together, hang papers on the wall, and generally act and react in comfort.

"Studies by Harvard's Levinson and other psychologists show that, for groups as well as individuals, a formal atmosphere inhibits the mood of 'relaxed concentration' necessary for the most productive work. Leaders usually get their best results when the participants feel comfortable in their surroundings. A reasonably attractive office may well be more suitable for most meetings than a formal conference room. The informality of any session, of course, must be balanced by a focused and organized meeting environment, with as few interruptions and distractions as possible. You should become sensitive to this balance, so that you will know when to relax and when to push for more work."

What's Available?

For everyday meetings, site selection is almost always restricted to what is readily available. This usually means a standard office, a larger office equipped for small meetings, or perhaps a conference room. For larger meetings, an auditorium or the company cafeteria, converted for the purpose, might be available. For big meetings, major presentations, or conferences that involve people from outside the organization or from distant offices, you may be able to select a restaurant with meeting facilities, a hotel, or a conference center.

For "routine" sessions, there will be times when you won't be able to get the meeting room you know is just right for your meeting. What then?

If only a small room is available, plan a small meeting or reschedule the meeting to a time when the right meeting room is available. Crowded rooms too small for the number of participants can be both psychologically and physically bad. The room quickly becomes stuffy. There is no room to move around or set up displays. Each of us is endowed with a sense of our own space and subconsciously resents intrusions on that space. When that resentment surfaces in an overcrowded meeting room, it can affect the tenor of discussion seriously and limit the work of those around the table.

If only a too-large room is available, some quick planning might solve the problem. You may be able to gather all participants at one end or in one corner of the room, with their backs to the open room, and achieve a sense of meeting unity. Or you might be able to use movable screens to partition the room and create a small room within the big room.

Meeting Site Criteria

When selecting the meeting site, take particular note of the following:

1. The size of the room.
2. The acoustics.
3. The lighting.
4. Distractions.
5. Access to the room.
6. Ventilation.
7. Room layout.

The Size of the Room

The room should fit the number of participants if possible. Eight people in an auditorium feel intimidated by the huge empty space. If you have ever walked into an auditorium presentation and found half a dozen people huddled in a knot at the front, you know the feeling. Sound echoes and hearing may be difficult. Concentration is difficult. While the presentation may be beautiful, it must overcome the cavernous surroundings and the lost feelings of the participants before it begins to communicate its message.

Big rooms discourage dialogue and induce an impersonal feeling. Some people, when it is their turn to talk, feel self-consciousness or develop stage fright in a room that is too big. Others find it hard to concentrate on the business of the meeting.

Some meetings in very small rooms, on the other hand, are like the 5 o'clock rush hour on a subway. Participants are squeezed elbow-to-elbow with no room for movement or for laying out materials on the table. They can become so occupied with thoughts of space that the subject for discussion gets only minor attention. The Standing Room Only sign is great for Broadway plays. It doesn't work well for meetings.

Acoustics

In big empty rooms, acoustics often are poor, especially if there are no drapes, carpeting, or other sound-absorbing materials to prevent echoes. Voices sound hollow or attenuated. Check any big room for acoustics before use because every participant should be able to hear everything that is said without straining. When participants can't hear well, they feel remote from the meeting and seldom really get into the swing of it.

If giving a presentation, stage a rehearsal in the room itself to test the acoustics. Try out the sound system if one is being used. If not, test your voice to see how you must project it to be heard. Remember, however, that the sound characteristics of a room change when it is full of people. An empty room may have an echo that disappears when a number of people are present. Their clothing dampens the sound, preventing reverberation and improving sound quality. Under some conditions, however, the clothing may absorb too much sound, so that hearing becomes more difficult.

The only safe procedure is to check the acoustics of any room with which you are unfamiliar before scheduling any meeting in it. If possible, visit the room when a meeting is in progress and people are present.

Lighting

Does the lighting in the room need to be controlled? For discussion meetings without presentations, control of the lighting usually isn't necessary. But when a presentation with visuals is part of the program, you may need to turn down the lighting so the visuals can be seen clearly. This isn't a problem with overhead projectors, but may be with a 35-mm slide, film, TV, or videotaped presentations.

Distractions

Meetings can be plagued with distractions—noises filtering in from the room next door, people coming and going as the meeting progresses, telephones ringing in the midst of the work. Meetings near airports may be interrupted by the roar of planes taking off and landing. Such distractions not only slow down the meeting but often interfere with discussion and prevent full interaction by the participants. Avoid rooms that have built-in distractions—thin walls that invite outside noises, for example. Make arrangements to eliminate telephones, coffee servers, note passers, and other predictable distractions. Incoming telephone calls should be intercepted by secretaries and messages can be delivered during the break or after the meeting.

If you have a choice, avoid rooms with windows, particularly rooms with windows facing into active work or recreation areas. You may lose the battle for the attention of the attendees.

One executive told us of a ground-floor meeting room at a hotel facing a sunny poolside area. He arrived to set up his meeting only to discover that preliminary judging for a statewide beauty contest would be going on around the pool while his meeting was in progress. The windows were draped and he quickly drew the drapes—but they proved to be partially transparent. The meeting participants would have ring-side seats at the contest judging. Being a good field general, the executive did a fast survey of his battlefield and found a solution. Commanding a platoon of hotel employees, he turned the room around by moving the podium to the wall opposite the windows. Now the participants would face the podium with their backs to the draped windows. By turning around, they could still see the activity around the pool—but most would find it embarrassing to be skewered by the steely eye of the presenter when they did.

Access to the Room

The best arrangement is to have the access to the room at the back so that those who come late or must leave early can do so without disturbing the meeting. If the podium is near the door, the meeting will falter momentarily every time the door is opened.

Ventilation

The air in a closed room full of people quickly becomes stuffy even if no one is smoking. Often even air conditioning can't keep the air fresh. Stuffy air and low levels of oxygen slow the activity of the participants, who soon begin to yawn and feel sleepy. Before any meeting, check to see that the room has sufficient ventilation—either mechanical or through windows. If only limited ventilation is possible, plan around the problem. This may mean restricting the number of people invited, making the meeting sessions shorter, with periods between them when the doors can be left open to ventilate the room, or finding another more suitable room.

The problem of mixing smoking and nonsmoking participants is real. Nonsmokers resent being asked to sit in a room full of stale smoke. Smokers often feel that they can't think clearly without their usual quota of cigarettes. There is no middle ground in this problem. Someone has to give up something. The best solution is to permit no smoking during the meeting. To accommodate participants who want to smoke, schedule a break during the meeting, when the smokers can leave the room for 10 minutes.

Today, the majority of smokers refrain from smoking at meetings out of consideration for the other members. But there always are some who don't think. For them, it is necessary to say, "No smoking during the meeting."

The Five Basic Room Arrangements

Five basic room arrangements have survived the test of time and thousands of meetings.

The Standard Office Setup

The vast majority of meetings are held in offices furnished with a desk and chairs. Meetings in offices work best when the chairs are arranged in a semicircle facing the desk, with the meeting leader behind the desk and the participants facing the desk. Depending on the size of the office, this arrangement is functional for up to six or at most eight participants. It is better for smaller groups. With the door closed, the average office feels crowded when occupied by eight people.

In larger offices with meeting space, the usual furnishings include a small conference table for up to eight people, or a "living room" arrangement of chairs around a coffee table for about the same number. The additional space in these offices makes them good for meetings up to perhaps 10. However, visual presentations are more difficult in these surroundings.

The Conference Table Setup (Figure 5.1*a*)

For small meetings where intense discussion is anticipated the standard arrangement is the conference table setup. The participants sit at a long conference table, with the meeting leader at the head of the table. This works with groups up to about 20. A round table permits a similar arrangement but is difficult for groups exceeding 12 simply because the table must be much bigger in area and occupies so much space when additional participants join the group.

The U-Shaped Table Setup
(Figures 5.1*b* and 5.2)

Ideal for meetings up to 30 people, the U-shaped table requires a room larger than the typical office or small conference room, but is an excellent setup for medium and large rooms for both discussion meetings and presentations. The open mouth of the U arrangement

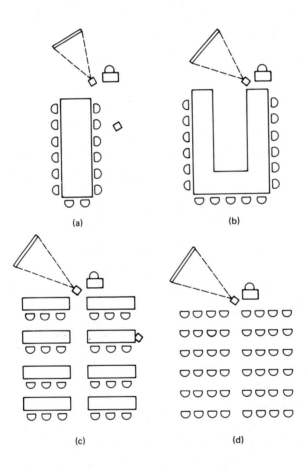

(a)

(b)

(c)

(d)

Figure 5.1 Typical meeting room arrangements. (*a*) Center table arrangement. Suitable for under 20 people. Promotes discussion. Best for long meetings. (*b*) U-Table arrangement. Suitable for 30 people or fewer. Promotes discussion. (*c*) Classroom arrangement. Suitable for any size audience. (*d*) Auditorium or theater arrangement. Suitable for any size audience.

faces the podium. The floor area near the podium provides room for screens and display setups.

The U-shaped table is good for smaller meetings of only six to eight as well as for larger meetings. The room with a U-table setup doesn't seem to have the empty feeling found in most larger rooms. For smaller meetings, participants simply move closer to the podium. In U-shaped arrangements, a microphone usually isn't necessary.

If the meeting leader prefers to sit at the meeting table instead of working from a podium, the U can be reversed, with the leader sitting in the center of the closed end of the U and the participants seated along either side. As a rule, participants should not be seated in the inside of the U. This creates two wings of people looking at each other. If space dictates a need for this arrangement, it can work, though it tends to limit discussion.

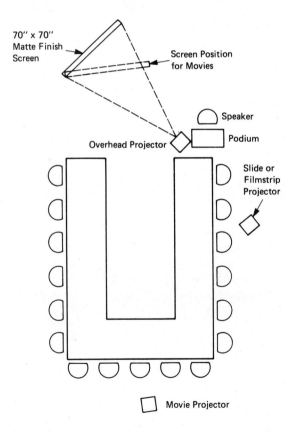

Figure 5.2 U-shape table arrangement. Best for discussion meetings and groups of 30 people or fewer.

The Classroom Setup
(Figure 5.1c)

In the classroom arrangement, the participants sit at tables and face a podium at the front of the room. It can be used in a room of any size, with the tables in rows across the room. If the tables are set at a slight angle, every participant has a clear view of the screen, which must be high enough so no one has to stretch to see it.

Every visual in a presentation should be easy to read from the back row. Many otherwise good presentations have failed because the visuals were difficult to read. In a later chapter, we will discuss how to design overhead transparencies and 35-mm slides for use in presentations, taking room size into account. The size and location of the screens are a factor, too. The most important points about display screens are the distance from the audience to the screen, the material from which the screen is made, and the size of the lettering on the screen. Readability often depends as much on the design of the visual as it does on screen placement.

The Theater (Figure 5.1d)

No tables are used in the theater arrangement. Attendees are seated in rows facing the podium and very large groups can be accommodated. Excellent for presentations and meetings for passing information to a lot of people, it doesn't work as well for discussion sessions because the theaterlike layout suggests passive rather than active participation. In this arrangement, the ability of the participants to hear the speaker and see the presentation material is of primary importance. A good sound system usually is necessary. Often, the podium and screens for visuals are raised so those in the back part of the room can see.

A variation on the theater setup is the amphitheater arrangement, with the rows of seats elevated in stair-step fashion and set in a semicircle facing the stage. Amphitheaters are excellent for very large meetings because of the near-perfect visibility. Figures 5.3 to 5.10 show various arrangements for different types of rooms.

Problem Meeting Rooms

Avoid meeting rooms with built-in problems. Very long, narrow rooms are difficult to use for any meeting except those employing long conference tables. Usually there isn't much room for moving about. In rooms with posts or columns, the speaker may not be able to see all the participants, and many participants won't be able to see the presentations comfortably. Rooms which are primarily used for other purposes, such as laboratories, sometimes are taken over for meetings, but they may have standing equipment and a furniture layout which makes their conversion to meeting use difficult.

Chairs

Meeting rooms need comfortable chairs. People forced to sit on hard folding chairs for any length of time soon find themselves distracted by their discomfort. If you expect full participation from people in meet-

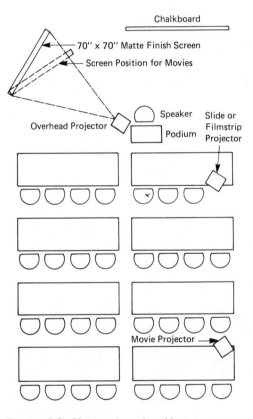

Figure 5.3 Horizontal work table arrangement. Suitable arrangement for any size group. Good for work-lecture combination groups of 15 to 100 people. Projection of screen size increases in larger rooms. Ceiling height should increase accordingly. Best for dissemination of information and for meetings at which little discussion is expected or desired.

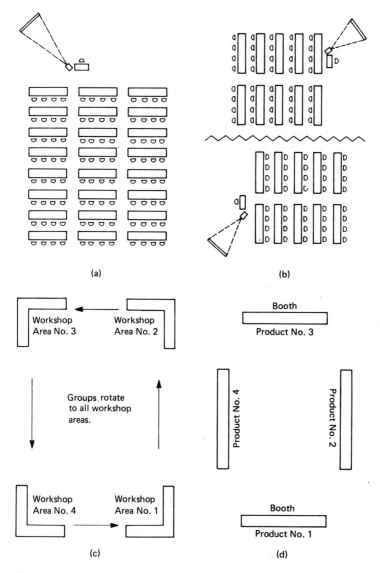

(a)

(b)

Workshop Area No. 3 ← Workshop Area No. 2

Groups rotate to all workshop areas.

Workshop Area No. 4 → Workshop Area No. 1

(c)

Booth

Product No. 3

Product No. 4

Product No. 2

Booth

Product No. 1

(d)

Figure 5.4 Four ways to use one room. (a) General session on first day. (b) Divided into two separate groups on second day. (c) Divided into four workshop groups on third day. (d) Divided to display new products to dealers and outside groups on fourth day.

ings, pay some attention to their basic needs—chairs which are comfortable when sat on for an hour or more, accommodations for writing so that notes can be taken, and room for people to get up and leave or walk to the podium without causing a disturbance.

Opinions differ on the question of comfort. Leslie This, in the *Small Meeting Planner*, suggests that "Physical facilities can be too plush and comfortable. Participants can concentrate better, participate more effectively and remain more mentally alert when there is a trace of discomfort. Chairs can be too comfortable. The chairs, table, and room can be distracting or too alluring. Meeting in a somber board room replete with formal, massive-legged mahogany table and pictures of austere organizational patriarchs staring from the walls can stifle informality and creativity."

Perhaps there is a middle ground—chairs which are almost comfortable, or not quite comfortable. We can agree that big leather-covered lounge chairs are too comfortable for meeting use. And straight-backed wooden folding chairs are too uncomfortable. The right kind of chair is somewhere between these two.

Figure 5.5 A medium-sized meeting room with U-shaped table arrangement. Notice the use of dual overhead projectors for a "stereo effect." This technique may be used, for example, to place the meeting agenda on one screen while using the second screen for the other visuals. Projecting the agenda can help keep a meeting on track.

Meeting Room Equipment

The average office is the site of most meetings but is seldom equipped to serve as such. The people just come in, sit down, and meet. However, as we have become more and more convinced that graphics are critical to good meetings, we have come to recommend that even the standard office be equipped for limited visual presentations.

No great amount of equipment is necessary, but the effectiveness of meetings held in the office can be increased through the ready availability of the right equipment. This might include a compact desktop overhead projector which takes very little room, an easel with a large paper pad, or a portable chalkboard. The overhead projector can be kept in a small cabinet when not in use and the easel or chalkboard can be folded and stored behind the door. Projections can be made directly on a light-colored wall or on a pull-down screen on the wall behind the desk.

The ordinary conference room should have an overhead projector and a screen, either wall-mounted or pull-down, as a part of its standard equipment. We have observed that when the equipment is there and ready, more people use it and the quality of the meetings improves.

In addition, the conference room might have two easels, one of which

Figure 5.6 A small room or portion of an office can be turned into a suitable meeting site using compact overhead projection equipment and careful placement of participants.

is of the roller type for mounting large displays. A cabinet in one corner is necessary for supply storage. A chalkboard is always useful, though not absolutely essential if large paper pads are mounted on one of the easels.

The larger conference or meeting room should have all of the same equipment plus a speaker's lectern or podium, an audio system, chairs for speakers or presenters, additional projection equipment such as a 35-mm slide projector and/or a motion picture projector.

With the rapid growth of video in business communication, a television set and a videotape player make an intelligent addition to any meeting room. For very large rooms, projection TV sets make sense. These have bright, clear pictures ranging in size up to 8 feet (diagonal measurement). Videotaped programs can be played through these sets.

Computer-related equipment has come into much greater use as electronic conferencing has increased. Most videoconferencing requires the use of specially equipped rooms. Major hotels and conference centers have videoconferencing facilities, but the type of equipment varies widely. To plan meetings in these facilities, check what they have. Is it compatible with your presentation materials or is special preparation necessary? Are trained operators necessary, or can your own people work the equipment? The best way to learn about the quality of results and problems connected with any of these facilities is to talk to someone who has used them.

Figure 5.7 This is a very large, executive-type meeting room with several pieces of visual aid equipment in evidence. There is room for a large number of participants around the U of the tables and in extra chairs on either wall. The pull-down screen shown is for use with the overhead projector, while the curtain covers a wide screen used for motion pictures—projected from a booth located behind the photographer—or slides. A videotape playback unit stands ready for use, along with a portable chalkboard.

Strategies in People Placement

The strategic placement of people around a conference table sometimes must be of concern to the meeting leader. For example, in a meeting of opposing groups, care should be taken that the two sides are not seated as groups. Group seating suggests that the battle lines have been drawn and can polarize the meeting, making a settlement of the differences more difficult. For the same reason, participants known to be obstructionists are best not seated as a group but should be distributed around the table. In either case, the group members will have their say without hindrance. The only purpose of the careful seating is to assure a better, more fluid discussion, and avoid polarized grouping and the resultant polarized group think.

However, directing the seating of people as they arrive at a meeting isn't easy. Place cards may be used at certain types of meetings; at other

Figure 5.8 A comfortably appointed auditorium can provide an appropriate setting for a large meeting. An auditorium, however, can be too comfortable, particularly if darkened for visual presentations. It may be difficult for participants to avoid the temptation to nod off during a presentation. Periodic adjustment of the lights will help keep your audience alert. Chairs with writing tablets built into the arms are also an obvious plus for note taking.

times, meeting leaders can simply ask or direct people to sit where they would prefer them.

Conference and Meeting Tables

The ideal conference or meeting room table is rectangular, usually 8 feet or more long and 3 to 4 feet wide. It provides ample working space for each participant yet maintains a sense of closeness without the feeling that personal space is threatened. These tables may be grouped in several effective layouts. Two or three can be placed in a straight line to make one long conference table, though care should be taken not to make the table too long or those at the "bottom" end will feel like they are out in the bleachers. The ideal maximum is about eight persons on each side of a long table, with the meeting leader sitting at one end, facing the group.

Tables can be arranged in an I-shape, U-shape, a classroom, or a theater set up (Figure 5.1). The U-shape is usually the most practical. T-shaped and H-shaped arrangements are not good for the viewing of visual presentations. In all cases, the objective is a good working arrangement for the most people considering the size of the room. The

Figure 5.9 An arrangement like this allows you to widen your audience for one or more presentations, through the use of extra chairs at one end, while still maintaining the closeness of the active participants, through the U arrangement of tables. This helps to utilize the space better in a large, long room. Note that there is a screen in the corner for the overhead projector and another can be pulled down from the ceiling for use with a movie projector or a slide projector. Product demonstrations frequently are given in this room.

critical thing is that the further you depart from face-to-face confrontation, the less intense will be the meeting.

Getting the Room Ready

The responsibility for getting the meeting room ready falls on the meeting leader (or, more often, on a secretary). The safest plan is to have all tasks performed by one person who works from a written checklist. If more than one person does the work, all should work from a master checklist so that everyone is aware of what has and has not been done.

Figure 5.10 If, as sometimes happens, the only available meeting room is too large for the group, be sure to move everyone up front to facilitate interaction. Note that the podium is offset to ensure that all participants have a clear view of the screen.

Tasks for readiness include:

1. Reserve the room for the day and time required.
2. Be certain that note pads, pencils, etc., are available.
3. Make arrangements for coffee or other refreshments.
4. Arrange for enough chairs for participants, and prepare place cards if required.
5. For presentations, check to see that equipment, such as overhead and slide projectors and sound equipment (amplifiers, microphones, and speakers), is in place and in working order. Each unit ought to be tested just before the meeting. Are projection lenses clean and ready? (One small but very valuable precaution: test electric outlets in the room as a part of meeting make-ready.)
6. Arrange to cut off telephones to the room and to take messages for participants.
7. Prepare a printed agenda and place one at each chair.
8. Check to see that reference material or handouts to be given to participants are in place on the meeting room table.
9. Check these small items in the conference room:
    Chalk and erasers for the chalkboard?
    Water and water glasses on the table?
    Paper pads mounted on the easel?
    Ashtrays, if smoking is permitted?
10. Availability of spare lamps and fuses for projection and other electrical equipment.
11. Flashlights or pointers available for presenters.
12. If lighting in the room is to be controlled, where are the controls? Do they work?

Distant Meetings

The preparation for any meeting held away from the office—in restaurants, hotels, or conference centers—is a three-step operation. Step one is to determine what equipment and supplies are available at the remote site and what must be brought from the office. Are overhead or 35-mm slide projectors on the site, or should they be brought in?

Step two, in the office, is the gathering of everything which must be taken to the remote site—copies of the agenda, all material to be distributed, scripts and visuals for presentations, and small items such as pads, pencils, etc.

Step three is performed at the meeting site, where every detail is checked against a prepared list, preferably the day before the meeting. It is never safe to leave details to the personnel employed by the hotel or conference center, for while they promise complete equipment and planning, slipups can and do occur.

Table and chair arrangements must be confirmed.

Equipment placement must be verified.

Operation of the equipment must be assured. If it doesn't work properly, the management must be notified in time to have it replaced.

If printed material or equipment must be transported or shipped to the site, who will receive it and how will it get to the meeting room?

The checker should have the name and phone number of the one person responsible for seeing to the arrival and placement of this equipment.

Signs needed at the site must be determined. Will participants be directed to the meeting room by signs or will they wander around trying to find it? If there are checkroom facilities, who will operate them?

Where are restrooms located?

Staffers to meet people at the meeting room door, check credentials, provide name tags, etc., must be arranged for.

Refreshment and meal schedules must be checked. If lunch is to be served, confirm the time and especially the place. Participants may need directions on how to find the dining area.

Anyone who has ever managed meetings quickly learns that disaster lurks in the small details. For example, the lamp in any projector, by Murphy's Law, will burn out in the middle of the most important part of a presentation. This will disturb the meeting to some degree, but if a replacement is immediately available, the break is not disastrous. However, if there is no replacement, or even worse, no one on the staff knows how to replace the lamp, the meeting may come to a quick, sometimes comical end.

To keep Mr. Murphy at bay, always check the room with the equipment placed exactly where it will be during the meeting. Do this as early as possible, preferably the day before. If it isn't done, we can almost guarantee that there will be no electric outlet adjacent to the spot where the equipment is to be used, that an extension cord will be necessary, and that no one will have one when it is needed. That is the way things seem to go at meetings.

To avoid problems, anticipate them. As Joseph Callanan advises in *Communicating*: "Pre-think emergencies. It's the very best way to avoid them. Put yourself through as many disaster situations as you can conjure up. Think through the event from preregistration to postadjournment, considering each step, each program, each arrangement. Try to think of the difficulties each attendee might encounter and the information he or she will need before, during, and after the conference. Of course, there will probably be some problems you couldn't possibly anticipate. Just keep moving forward as best you can."

Summary

The physical environment of a meeting has a significant effect on the psychological environment and thus on the outcome of the meeting. What is needed is an appropriate site of the right size that is properly equipped. Leaders get best results when the participants feel comfortable in their surroundings and can feel the mood of "relaxed concentration" necessary for the most productive work. Formal settings are not conducive to getting down to intensive work.

When selecting the meeting site, consider the following:

1. Size of the room. The room should fit the number of participants.
2. The acoustics. Every participant must hear everything that is said without straining.
3. Lighting—controllable as necessary.
4. Distractions to be eliminated before the meeting starts.
5. Access to the room—from the back, not the front.
6. Good ventilation.
7. A room layout suited to the room and the purpose of the meeting.

Meeting Room Equipment

Meeting rooms, including regular offices, should have minimal visual equipment in place. Effectiveness of office meetings can be increased through the use of equipment such as a compact desktop overhead projector, an easel with a large paper pad, or a portable chalkboard.

Readiness Checklist

The responsibility for getting the meeting room ready falls on the meeting leader or a secretary working from a written checklist. Tasks for assuring readiness include:

1. Room reservations for the day and time required.
2. Note pads, pencils, etc., available.
3. Coffee or other refreshments arranged for.
4. Chairs for participants. Place cards if necessary.

5. Equipment for presentations in place and in working order, tested just before the meeting.

6. Telephones to the room cut off.

7. Printed agenda at each chair.

8. Reference data and other handouts in place on the meeting table.

9. Small items for the conference room:
   - Chalk and erasers.
   - Water and water glasses.
   - Paper pad on the easel.
   - Ashtrays, if smoking is permitted.
   - Spare lamps and fuses for projection equipment.
   - Flashlights or pointers for presenters.

10. Location and operation of lighting controls.

6

Using
Leadership
Skills

To be a meeting leader, you must do more than just occupy the chair at the head of the table. Lawrence C. McQuade, executive vice president of W. R. Grace & Co., once pointed out in a *Forbes Magazine* article that if a meeting is unsuccessful, the fault is squarely that of the person running the meeting. McQuade viewed the meeting chair's role as a balancing act. "You have to get all the imagination and ideas and experience that you can into a meeting," he said. "In doing that, you have to be careful not to let people run on too long, so you have to have some disciplinary rules. The chairman must crystallize the main points as the meeting goes along and sum up for people. The summation must then move toward action."

Every meeting, from the smallest to the largest, requires leadership. There are three phases to any meeting. Phase one is the organizational period, in which the meeting is called, the agenda prepared, the room organized, the invitations issued, etc. The ability to organize is part of leadership. Phase two is the meeting itself. In this phase, the leader fronts the meeting, steers it through its body of work, and brings it to a successful conclusion. Phase three is the postmeeting follow-up.

In previous chapters we have covered most of phase one and examined the meeting from its inception as an idea up to the time the participants enter the meeting room. The preparation required imagination, investigation, attention to detail, sound common sense. It did not, however, involve the convener in such things as stage presence, face-to-face confrontations, verbal leadership, and the other skills required to actually conduct a group of participants through an agenda to get something accomplished.

Leadership Can Be Learned

Leaders are made, not born. The skills needed to run a meeting are not inherited. They can be acquired through practice and a sense of commitment to being a good manager. Some may argue with the idea, but the majority of chief executives believe that meeting skills can indeed be learned, as witnessed by the fact that in recent years, more than half of the *Fortune 500* companies hired outside experts to teach these skills to their executives and managers.

Meeting leadership should be viewed as a management skill to be acquired. There is no mysticism and no special talent involved. To be a meeting leader requires neither the silver tongue of a keynote speaker, nor the stage presence of a world-class actor. The required skills are no more difficult to acquire than those of making up a departmental budget. They are best learned over a period of time through concentration and practice. Each meeting presided over or attended represents an opportunity to put a skill or two to work, or to sharpen a skill already acquired.

Showmanship and Charisma

In assessing skills of a leader, leadership is sometimes confused with showmanship. Some people have a natural flair for putting on a show in front of a group. Their tongues are agile, they have stage presence, and they instantly engage the audience's attention. More than one manager has envied this flair in his or her peers. A manager who is tongue-tied in front of a group assumes that he or she hasn't the talent for meeting leadership. This isn't true. This manager, like many others, just doesn't have very much ham in his or her makeup, and while a little ham may be helpful, it is not an important quality of a leader.

The qualities needed by a business meeting leader include a depth of knowledge of the subject; presence of mind and the ability to think on one's feet as a meeting progresses—especially when it takes unexpected turns; and the skill to verbally manage and discipline the participants. The leader must be able to elicit cooperation from friend and foe alike, walk a middle path through controversy, and bring dissident parties together. The leader must be able to view the subject of the meeting objectively and bring this view to those who see only small parts of the problem. A leader must be tactful in the handling of people and their problems, and must approach every problem with a great sense of logic.

Some people have that other elusive quality, charisma. When they take the front position in any gathering, they generate feelings of enthusiasm in the audience. Charisma radiates from people with widely different characteristics and produces widely different results, both good and bad. Roosevelt, Churchill, Hitler, and Kennedy all had an abundance of charisma. Charisma is mysterious, and no one has ever determined what it is made of or how to acquire it. Its chief characteristic is that it makes people want to follow the leader who has it.

For a business leader, however, charisma, like showmanship, isn't necessary. A business meeting isn't called for the purpose of developing a following—or shouldn't be. Persons with charisma or showmanship do not necessarily have the other important qualities of leadership required for business meetings. In most cases, people with natural charisma or showmanship must learn the fundamentals of running a meeting in the same way as those of us without these attributes.

Stage Presence

A meeting leader may not need charisma or showmanship, but does need *stage presence*. Stage presence might be defined as a demeanor of calm competent confidence—the three Cs—exhibited by a leader before any audience. These qualities can be learned through practice.

Calmness

Nervousness before a group stems from two sources. One is the adrenaline which automatically pumps into the bloodstream whenever the body faces a crisis—nature's way of preparing the body to react quickly in an emergency. As soon as the emergency is over, the adrenaline level in the blood returns to normal. Most speakers feel an anticipatory rush of adrenaline a few minutes before they go on stage. Through experience they learn that the excess of adrenaline lasts only a few minutes and subsides shortly after the presentation begins. One veteran speaker says, "All I have to do is survive the first two minutes at the podium. After that, my adrenaline gets down to a manageable level."

Those just becoming leaders should recognize that nervousness in front of a group is not some kind of physical or psychological deficiency. It is a normal, healthy reaction to what the body sees as an emergency situation.

The second source of nervousness is uncertainty. Speakers or leaders who feel uncertain about the subject, the quality of the presentation, or of their own appearance will be nervous. The obvious cures are to (1) know the subject thoroughly; (2) take the time to prepare a solid presentation; and (3) be careful of appearance.

Competence

Nothing helps a meeting leader more than a sure sense of competence in the subject at hand. This comes through the simple process of doing one's homework. Wise meeting leaders never attempt to front a meeting without thoroughly reviewing all available material on the subject. They prepare by knowing what the meeting should accomplish and what is needed to make that accomplishment possible. They understand, in advance, what problems might arise and have thought them through.

Confidence

Confidence is in large part a by-product of competence. The leader who knows the subject matter and objectives of the meeting has reason to be confident. Confidence is, essentially, an outward expression of an inner sense of security.

Newcomers to leadership often try to establish the three Cs through strong self-control. They believe nervousness can be overcome by sheer willpower. However, preparation and practice are the real wellsprings of leadership. Confidence and a sense of competence come from feeling secure about the subject of the meeting, about the presentation, and about the agenda of the meeting. Confidence creates a kind of charisma, and meeting participants look for it in any meeting leader. When they see it, they, too, feel confident about the outcome of the meeting, and their participation improves.

The Executive's View of Self

Executives agree, according to Herbert Mayer in *Fortune*, that "what screws up so many meetings is *everybody else's* inability to perform effectively and efficiently before an audience." Mayer says, "Human nature being what it is, the executive has not yet been born who will concede that he, personally, is a bust at meetings; that he himself has ever lost control of a group or, worse, wasted time at somebody else's meeting by rambling on and on, entranced by the music of his own voice."

Seasoned executives, having run and attended more meetings than they care to remember, tend to view themselves as experts in the meeting business. In some cases, they are. All too frequently, however, they are not. They *are* skillful executives but have either lost or never had well-developed skills as meeting leaders. The 3M Business Meetings Team, in working with top executives, can only ask them to sit in on our training sessions, honestly review their skills, and upgrade themselves when they find they are a bit short in the skills department.

Control: The Basic Skill

Leadership, according to one statesman, is "the art of getting someone else to do something that you want done because he wants to do it." In practical terms, this means that a leader knows how to inspire and motivate those he or she leads. In business meetings, this isn't done through motivational speeches or half-time pep talks, but by competently exercising the standard leadership roles in calling and running meetings.

The meeting leader's most important roles are those of moderator and facilitator—controller of the meeting's pace and thrust. Ideally, the leader keeps things on course, maintains an orderly progression, and steers the ship through the shoals and sandbars. In mission-oriented meetings, where problems are to be solved or policies hammered out, the leader's job is to generate discussion, lead it toward a resolution, then pull everything together in a final summary. The leader's own ideas and expertise can be contributed, but only if he or she steps away from the chair—at least figuratively—and speaks out as a participant, not as the leader.

In presentation meetings, the leader is more of a coordinator, introducing the presenters, managing the time of the meeting, interpreting, explaining, and summarizing for the audience as necessary. The task is no less important than in a deliberative session, but it is different. Control of presentation meetings often is not quite as direct, since others are making the presentations, but it must be exercised.

In either type of meeting, the basic skill employed is *control*. The leader must know how to control the meeting, and the participants must be aware of this control. Sometimes the control is exercised in subtle ways, sometimes it is blatant. We will discuss the individual techniques shortly.

How to Act Like a Leader

Well-practiced meeting leaders walk into the room with calm confidence, proceed to the leader's chair, arrange papers and notes, and then turn to the group *as the leader*. They exude the idea that they know the purpose of the meeting and communicate it to everyone else in the room. One reason a meeting leader should never be late is that it is very difficult to exude calm confidence while rushing in late and hastily apologizing, at the same time scattering papers on the table and trying to find the meeting agenda. In this case, the battle for leadership is lost before the meeting starts.

Good presenters and speakers approach the podium at a medium pace and take a few deliberate seconds to arrange the script and adjust the microphone if there is one. They let themselves get settled in. They then look at the audience and hold the gaze for a few seconds. All of this gives the adrenaline a little time to subside and reduces any stage fright or nervousness. It also gives the audience an opportunity to prepare to listen.

During the talk, they consciously strive to keep their speech slow, recognizing that most people talk too fast when speaking in public. The best speech is made at a pace about half that of normal conversation. The slow pace permits good enunciation, enabling the audience to hear and understand every word.

The Rules of Good Meeting Leadership

Briefly, there are good guides for a meeting leader.

1. Know the audience.
2. Anticipate meeting attitudes and positions.
3. Speak the language of the participants.
4. Appeal to the interests of the participants.
5. Know precisely what needs to be said—the result of a good premeeting organization.
6. Present any materials simply and concisely. If possible, use visual aids to enhance communication.

7. Maintain a firm, confident, positive demeanor.

8. Speak at a moderate pace in a well-modulated voice that is loud enough to be heard easily around the table.

9. Avoid distracting mannerisms.

10. Work to stimulate group discussion.

11. Consider the suggestions and opinions of everyone.

12. Follow the agenda step by step, and keep the others aware of it.

13. Never allow control of the meeting to slip away.

How to Open a Meeting

The good meeting leader opens with a brief statement of the purpose of the meeting. A common error is to open the meeting with a long statement that rambles into the background of the subject and attempts to present information the group needs to do its work. A leader following this course is guilty of dominating the floor and runs the risk of diminished response from the participants. If either background material or information statements are necessary, the most effective method is to call on others around the table for them. Brief presentations for this purpose can be scheduled on the agenda.

If, in the opening statement, the leader presents personal opinions about the subject of the meeting—before any discussion by the panel— those around the table begin to hear the loud whistle of a locomotive. They feel they are about to be railroaded into a decision. They suspect the meeting is strictly to approve the leader's ideas, not to arrive at a group judgment, and they quickly lose interest.

The well-constructed opening statement is short and to the point: "This meeting has been called to. . . . " Then the leader makes the role of the participants clear. "Our job is to determine. . . . " With these items out of the way, the leader then deftly throws the ball to someone else: "Bill has been in earlier meetings and knows the background of the problem. He can paint it in for you. Then Grace, who also has been close to the project, will take about 5 minutes to give us the latest data. After that, we can begin our discussion."

This opening accomplishes a lot. It clearly establishes meeting leadership. It indicates the job to be done and the participation that is expected. Most important, perhaps, it demonstrates that the leader has done some serious planning and has a clear understanding of the meeting's objectives. (Obviously, this leader will have talked to Bill and Grace a day or so before the meeting to give them time to get their presentations together.)

Techniques for Leading a Meeting

Discussion is the heart of every good meeting. The two quickest ways to turn off discussion in a meeting are for the leader to (a) dominate the discussion and (b) to never ask for participation.

During the meeting, to generate discussion and to maintain control, the leader should:

1. Ask open-ended questions . . . questions that can't be answered with a yes or no.

2. Reinforce statements made by participants that are on target with meeting objectives.

3. Redirect any questions aimed at the chair to others in the group.

4. Carefully use relevant examples out of his or her own experience to encourage the group to think along similar lines.

5. Ignore off-target remarks. Discussion only reinforces them.

6. Ask questions, either of an individual or of the whole group, that relate to the task at hand.

7. Restate relevant points of the agenda when the discussion veers from objectives.

8. Firmly put down participants who dominate any discussion by asking them to let others speak. One way is to say, "I understand your point. Now let's hear from someone else on it."

9. When an off-the-track subject looms as important, ask the group's opinion as to whether it should be added to the agenda now or at a later meeting.

10. As the group moves through the agenda, keep it on track by offering quick summaries. "Okay, so far we have determined that . . . ."

Leadership Cautions

Control can be subtle. Little things can affect the tenor of a meeting and cause it to come apart or lose its momentum. They also can destroy the respect the participants should have for the leader. Some of these are:

1. The leader resents a question and shows it. Questions, even unwanted ones, should be encouraged. The unwanted ones can be handled.

2. The leader gets into the discussion and monopolizes it.

3. The leader plays the role of the comic. A little humor is welcome at most meetings, but the leader with aspirations to be a stand-up comic soon reduces a serious meeting to a vaudeville show.

4. The leader puts a participant down, especially with a personal remark. There will always be problem participants, but a public put-down on a personal level is never the right method of managing one. Take the participant aside during a break and ask for cooperation.

5. The leader permits an argument to develop between participants. When a discussion gets past a certain point and becomes an argument, it is essential to step in and get the meeting back on the agenda.

6. The leader looks confused, unprepared, or unknowledgeable. Coming to a meeting unprepared, for a leader, is worse than not coming at all. If there hasn't been time to prepare, the best course is to postpone the meeting until the preparations can be taken care of.

How to Close a Meeting

The leader must recognize the right time to bring a meeting to a close. When all items on an agenda have been covered, there is a tendency for participants to begin recapping. They go back to earlier points, bring up new discussion, and develop a rehash of the meeting. If this tendency goes unchecked, a meeting can easily run an extra hour. A leader must realize when all pertinent discussion has been completed and communicate it by saying something like, "Well, we've covered all the items on the agenda." If the meeting was to make a decision, set policy, or determine a course of action, the leader should now sum up the consensus with a statement such as, "From what has been said, we all feel that . . . ," and finish by asking if all agree with the statement.

Sometimes there is quick agreement. At other times, clarification and perhaps additional discussion is necessary—and should be permitted. The main objective in these closing moments is to arrive at a conclusion that everyone understands and agrees with. The danger is that discussion at this time may develop into prolonged debate, so the leader must maintain control and keep trying to phrase a final statement that wins general agreement.

In the final statement, the leader should spell out the action or decision at which the group had arrived and relate it to the stated meeting objective. Did the group meet the objective? Or was the objective only partially met?

During a meeting, people often are assigned further work. They are asked to dig up information or explore another facet of the problem for the group. Usually these assignments require a later memo to all group members or a report at the next meeting. As a part of the closing statement, the meeting leader should clearly outline what action is expected, who is to carry it out, and what form the report will take.

Finally, if another meeting on the subject is to be scheduled, the leader should state the fact now. If possible, a date and time should be set, subject to change later if necessary.

In the case of a presentation meeting, the leader's closing statement should be a quick summary of what has been presented, and, if possible, a statement relating the content of the presentation to ongoing work.

Meeting Minutes

Minutes and meeting reports are always necessary for important formal meetings, but often are ignored in informal daily meetings. It is assumed that everyone will remember what the final outcome was and what assignments were made. Later, the participants find themselves saying to each other, "I thought we took care of that at the meeting," or "Wasn't Joe supposed to get that information for the next meeting?"

A sure cure for such postmeeting problems is a brief set of minutes. Some leaders ask one of the participants to jot down notes during the meeting, and they then use the notes to dictate a memo which is sent to all participants following the meeting. A simpler way is to use a regular form, such as the 3M Meeting Action Plan, illustrated in Chapter 5, or to take notes right on the agenda sheet, jotting down points of discussion, assignments, and final conclusions beside each agenda item. This can be used as a guide in the preparation of the final memo.

Whatever method is used, the leader has the responsibility of seeing that minutes or a report in some form are in the hands of all participants within a day or two of the meeting. The meeting is not actually over until a set of minutes is in the hands of everyone who should have it.

Personal Leadership Evaluation

Whether you are new to the corporate structure and just beginning a career of meetings, or have been running them for 20 years, a personal evaluation of your own skills is an excellent idea. The evaluation needs to be honest, for there is little point in deceiving yourself. Here are some questions to answer:

- What are my strong points?
- What are my weak points?
- How effective was I at the last meeting? What was the best thing I did? The worst thing?

To answer these questions, look at the way you prepared for the last meeting and how well you organized it. Think about your performance during the meeting and how it might be improved.

Did you get good participation? Did you encourage or discourage it? Did you listen to the other participants? How well did you control troublesome participants? Were better ways available? Did you follow the agenda and keep the meeting rolling? Did you close with a good summary statement and a review of action assignments? Did everyone leave feeling that they knew what had been accomplished and what had to be done next? Did you follow with a meeting report to all participants?

With these thoughts in mind, ask yourself:

- What part of my meeting technique can I improve?
- Can I do it myself, or should I take some training?

Finally, break down any improvements needed into individual elements. Concentrate on these one at a time. Don't attempt to overhaul the whole ship in one trip to the drydock. By simply being aware of needed improvements, you will find that your meeting performance improves quickly.

Podium Pointers for Presenters

The quickest way to distract an audience during a presentation is through odd mannerisms. Sometimes these mannerisms are the result of nervousness or they may be unconscious little habits we display without being aware of them—such as tugging an earlobe, playing with a wristwatch, or rattling bracelets. We have collected a few of these distracting mannerisms here. No doubt you'll recognize friends of yours as you read—and perhaps might even note a habit or two of your own.

The Gripper

This person hangs on to the podium for dear life and would fall flat if the podium weren't there. The Gripper telegraphs nervousness by displaying white knuckles. Nervousness is common to everyone who ever stepped in front of a crowd. Bob Hope once said that if he didn't have butterflies in his stomach before going on, even after 50 years of performing, he knew something was wrong. Fortunately, once you are launched into your speech, the adrenaline slows down and the nervousness evaporates. One way to help the process is to forget that you are talking to a large audience and concentrate on one person in about the third row. Talk to that person a few seconds, then move your eyes to another individual, and then another. If you have Gripper tendencies, practice standing back from the podium.

The Musician

This bird is male and nervously rattles keys or coins in his pocket. There is a female version who enjoys twirling beads or playing with chains or jewelry. It isn't long before the audience becomes more interested in the musical performance than the other one. A simple solution: empty pockets and remove noisy jewelry before getting up in front of the audience.

The Weakling

The weakling collapses all over the podium and looks about to fall in a heap. As near as we can tell, weaklings get this way by trying to relax—and overdoing it. Somehow, they convey a lack of firmness by this posture. Audiences aren't inclined to take them seriously. Cure: Practice the presentation without a podium and become accustomed to standing on your own two feet.

The Orator

Even though great oratory has been out of style for a long time, there are still those who want to make spellbinding speeches. Orators are boring. In a business meeting, people want things to keep moving. The big oration, and that includes those by presidents and board chairpersons as well as the rest of us, is a big dead pause in an otherwise well-paced meeting. The applause at the end of an oration is not a recognition of a good speech but a celebration that the speech is over.

The Pacer

Pacers remind the audience of caged lions. They prowl back and forth across the stage as if trying to work off excess energy. As a pacer performs, the audience looks like the swivel-headed fans watching a tennis match. The speaker's constant movements get the listeners' attention though the words may not. Some controlled movement is an effective way of making a speech feel alive; excessive movement diminishes its impact.

The Bon Voyageur

Bon voyageurs wave their hands as if their boat was about to pull out on a voyage to Europe. Someone once taught them to move their hands for emphasis while speaking—and they took the instruction very seriously. The only cure is to concentrate on resting the hands on the edge of the podium or comfortably at one's side most of the time. Hand movements should be used for occasional emphasis—and if used only occasionally, can be very effective.

The Reader

Many people read speeches and do quite well at it. But most readers look down at the script and read it in a monotone. Because their voices are projected back at the paper and not toward the audience, they are difficult to hear. They seldom raise their eyes to the audience and almost always fail to make good personal contact. They seldom establish any personal identity, remaining just a voice to the audience. This reduces the impact of whatever they have to say. The right way to read a speech from a script is to look at the audience frequently, and to glance down at the script only to see the next couple of lines before speaking them. A good speaker gives the talk a feeling of naturalness and injects emotion or enthusiasm into it—even when reading it line for line from the paper.

Curing These Bad Habits

On the way to becoming a good meeting leader or presenter, look yourself over for signs of any of these bad habits. If you find some, work studiously on getting rid of them. Good leaders or presenters assume an easy, natural stance in front of a podium, standing erect with hands sometimes gently resting on the podium, sometimes gesturing. During the talk, they change stance occasionally, and even walk a bit near the podium. All their actions communicate the feeling that they are comfortable, relaxed, in command of the situation, and know what they are talking about.

Meeting Annoyances

Little annoyances disturb the concentration of people in a meeting.
Leaders and participants alike can be guilty of being one or more of the
following:

The Pencil People

Some people find pencils absolutely fascinating. They bounce the points
on the tabletop, usually in some kind of rhythm. They twirl them or roll
them or examine them for fleas. Whatever it is they do, Pencil People
can really be distracting in an intense meeting. Both leaders and
participants can be guilty of this.

The Doodler

Doodlers concentrate best when making elaborate drawings. Unfortunately, Doodlers don't look like they are concentrating on the meeting
but on their artistic endeavors. There is nothing really wrong with
doodling, and inveterate doodlers insist that doodling focuses their
thoughts. Perhaps. But we've always felt that taking meeting notes for
later reference might be more productive.

The Commentator

Every meeting seems to have a commentator who likes to inject asides
and offhand comments into the discussion. Sometimes the commentator
is trying to be funny; other times, he or she must get a word in even
though the floor belongs to someone else at the moment. Usually it is a
ploy to gain attention. Commentators seldom destroy a discussion, but
they certainly don't help it. We've noticed that commentators tend to be
one-sided. If someone injects an aside comment when they are speaking—watch out! They quickly remind everyone that they have the floor.
Both meeting leaders and participants can be guilty of this.

The Critic

The Critic can be heard all through the meeting, usually *sotto voce*. The
Critic's little gripes float in under the discussion. First, the chairs are
hard. Next the air is stale. Then the water isn't cold. Critics are most
evident when meetings run long.

The Conversationalist

This is the attendee who has important things to say to the person sitting next to him or across the table. It seldom has anything to do with the subject of the meeting, and it obviously can't wait until the meeting is over. The chair's only recourse may be to tap a water glass with a spoon to call for order—or to direct a question at the offenders. Conversationalists seldom really participate in a meeting. They just attend.

Summary

The art of leading a meeting and the attributes of leadership can be learned through observation and practice. A meeting leader doesn't need charisma or showmanship, but should develop a demeanor of calm, competent confidence when fronting meetings.

The major element of leadership is the ability to control the meeting's discussion and keep the participants to the agenda.

The leader generates discussion and maintains an orderly progression in mission-oriented meetings, leads it toward a resolution, then pulls everything together in a final summary. In presentation meetings, the leader serves as a coordinator, introducing the presenters, managing the time of the meeting, interpreting, explaining, and summarizing for the audience as necessary.

The Rules of Meeting Leadership

1. Know the audience.
2. Anticipate meeting attitudes and positions.
3. Speak the language of the participants.
4. Appeal to the interests of the participants.
5. Know precisely what needs to be said—the result of good premeeting organization.
6. Present any materials simply and concisely using visual aids if possible.
7. Maintain a firm, confident, positive demeanor.
8. Speak at a moderate pace in a well-modulated voice, loud enough to be heard easily around the table.
9. Avoid distracting mannerisms.
10. Stimulate group discussion.
11. Consider the suggestions and opinions of everyone.
12. Follow the agenda and keep the others aware of it.
13. Never allow control of the meeting to slip away.

The meeting leader's most important roles are those of moderator and facilitator—controller of the meeting's pace and thrust. The leader keeps things on course, maintains an orderly progression, and steers the discussion through rough spots. In meetings where problems are to be solved or policies hammered out, the leader generates discussion, leads it toward a resolution, and then pulls everything together in a final summary. The basic skill employed is *control*. The leader must know how to control the meeting. Sometimes the control is exercised in subtle ways, sometimes it is blatant.

Techniques for Leading a Meeting

Discussion is the heart of every good meeting. During the meeting, to generate discussion and to maintain control, the leader should:

1. Ask open-ended questions that can't be answered with a yes or no.
2. Reinforce statements made by participants that are on target with meeting objectives.
3. Redirect any questions aimed at the chair to others in the group.
4. Carefully use relevant examples out of his or her own experience to encourage the group to think along similar lines.
5. Ignore off-target remarks. Discussion only reinforces them.
6. Ask questions, either of an individual or of the whole group, that relate to the task at hand.
7. Restate relevant points of the agenda when the discussion veers from objectives.
8. Firmly put down participants who dominate any discussion by asking them to let others speak.
9. Ask the group's opinion when an off-the-track subject enters the discussion as to whether it should be added to the agenda now or held for a later meeting.
10. Offer quick summaries as the group moves through the agenda items.

7

The Skills of Participation

" . . . What they need is the ability to think on their feet, to make their cases clearly and briefly, to convince doubters that their fears are groundless, to disagree agreeably, and above all to shut up when there is nothing more to say."

This is the way Herbert Meyer, writing in *Fortune Magazine*, summed up what meeting participants need to know.

Being a business meeting participant is work and carries with it a responsibility. People who attend business meetings are vital parts of a working team trying to reach a common objective. To be able and worthy participants, they must exercise a variety of skills. Add to Meyer's list of abilities some others: a good participant needs to know how to listen, how to join a discussion, how to make a contribution, how to join with others in arriving at a clear-cut decision, and how to disagree constructively.

The primary responsibility of a meeting participant is to contribute. No participant should attend a meeting to sit in as a more or less interested spectator, occupying the space without taking part in the ongoing action. As pointed out in earlier chapters, there are good reasons to be an active participant in meetings: (1) to contribute to the success of the company, (2) by contributing to the company, to gain personal recognition and eventual promotion, and (3) by active participation, to learn more about the department, the company, and the industry.

Tips for Meeting Participants

In an article in *Supervisory Management*, Edward F. Konczal, then Staff Manager for the AT&T Long Lines, Service Costs and Rates Department, offered a worthwhile series of tips for meeting participants.

- Question the need for your attendance at any meeting. You should be able to justify the time you spend at it. If you are asked to attend a meeting that has limited bearing on your work, call the meeting manager to find out why you were asked to participate. If there is a need for you to attend but you have a schedule conflict, find out more about what is to be discussed so you can determine where your time is best spent.

- Do your homework. If you expect to have something to offer at the meeting, make sure you understand the purpose of the meeting and the agenda items. Prepare your thoughts and organize the comments you plan to share at the meeting. Your performance and the productivity of the meeting will be enhanced by preparation.

- Speak up. Question items that you feel need clarification. Check the accuracy of the material presented. You may have an insight or be aware of data or information that could correct certain misconceptions. Meetings have a tendency to develop a "group-think" mentality, and you could set the meeting on a productive course. A certain amount of conflict helps to stop group-think, but at all costs, avoid conflict that results in wasted time and unnecessary emotional strain. When disagreement arises, ask questions to clarify the issues and state the other person's view to ensure there is no misunderstanding. Be intelligent enough to point out the value of suggestions you know are right. Admit your mistakes and don't emphasize those of others. Back off and ask for a conference at another time if the discussion is going nowhere.

- The emphasis should be on problem solving. Offer information, thoughts, and suggestions that move the meeting in a productive direction, and don't waste time with irrelevant anecdotes and long-winded monologues. Success in most managerial functions depends on influencing others. Knowing where to place a humorous remark is one of the best tools for that. In the mounting tension of some meetings, your sense of humor could be the best vehicle to keep the group moving.

- Never surprise the boss. If you have a new proposal to offer at the meeting that will influence the work of your group, be sure to review it with your boss before the meeting. Your proposal may be outstanding, but it should be screened with the boss, who may have additional insight into where the proposal fits into the purpose of the meeting.

How to Listen

All of us know how to listen—or at least think we do. After all, we do it every day in every waking hour. At the same time, we all regularly experience the problem of talking to people who don't listen to what we say. "I told him what I wanted, but he didn't listen," is a complaint we all make pretty often. It demonstrates that we understand the difference between *hearing* and *listening*. To hear is not necessarily to listen. Hearing is a physical act; listening is the act of hearing coupled with comprehension.

The ability to listen well is the first and most necessary skill needed by a meeting participant, but its value isn't restricted to meetings. It is a useful asset throughout business and personal life because everyone likes a good listener. Good listeners compliment the person they listen to. In effect, the listener says, "I listen to you because what you have to say is worth my time and attention."

Generally, listening is easy when we are relaxed and untroubled but not so easy when we have other things to think about—and then it can be just plain hard work. The test of good listeners comes when they can focus attention and listen attentively in spite of a mind full of other thoughts. Commanding the full attention of a busy mind for very long is difficult. However, in spite of the difficulties, it is possible to become a successful listener—one who knows how to shut out other thoughts and focus attention on what is being said. With practice, good listening becomes a habit.

Guidelines for Good Listening

The greatest barrier to good listening is inattentiveness. The following rules for good listening actually are hints on how to be attentive.

1. *Establish frequent eye contact with the meeting leader or speaking participants.* This helps to focus attention on what is being said and tends to block out distractions that would otherwise interfere.

2. *Always try to hear the ideas—not the words—being presented.* Some

speakers are deft at getting their ideas across; most are not. Try to cut through the verbal undergrowth that often surrounds an idea—to get to a real understanding.

3. *Block out thoughts that aren't a part of the meeting.* Work and personal problems are always standing in the wings of your mind, waiting for the opportunity to take the center stage. If your attentiveness to the meeting subject waivers a bit, they may come dancing out, and it usually takes an act of will power to send them back. With practice, mental discipline of this type becomes a habit that affects positively everything you do.

4. *Work at increasing your attention span.* Psychologists have made various estimates of the average human attention span. While their conclusions vary, their research demonstrates that most of us have surprisingly short attention spans. The reason is not that we are intellectually impaired but that we have so many things we either must or want to think about that our minds tend to jump from one subject to the next. Like the kid with a quarter in a candy store, we hardly know which jar of goodies to concentrate on.

5. *Take notes.* The very act of taking a pencil in hand and jotting down notes of key words during a discussion helps to keep the attention focused on the meeting. In particular, make notes of questions that come to mind during a discussion. In complex discussions, a set of notes for reference is helpful in following the twists and turns of the debate.

6. *Ignore a speaker's faulty delivery or lapses in logic.* It is easy to distract one's own listening by dwelling on how badly a speaker is making a point. A better way is to attempt to understand what the speaker is saying even if it seems muddled, then ask questions or restate your understanding of what was said when the speaker has finished.

The mental discipline required to eject extraneous thoughts requires effort. In the first few tries, the span of undivided attention must be refocused frequently. But with practice, the span increases until reasonably good control is gained over the mind. Like the weightlifter who gradually increases the amount of iron he or she can pump, your span of undivided attention grows longer with practice and control is achieved with less effort.

Racing Ahead

A deceptive kind of inattention occurs when participants are so involved in a meeting discussion that their minds race ahead of the speaker to deal with new ideas. As their minds jump ahead, they often miss the point of the discussion taking place at the moment. Racing ahead is a good sign, an indication that participants want to contribute, but it needs to be brought under control because too much may be missed while it is going on. The best solution is to listen attentively and jot down one- or two-word reminders of fresh ideas as they occur. *It is possible to listen carefully and think ahead at the same time,* as long as your attention doesn't swerve from the meeting to pursue one of the new ideas to the exclusion of everything else.

How to Join the Discussion

Participants are expected to find the flaws in poor ideas, expand on growing ideas, and contribute fresh ideas of their own. An active, well-prepared participant does these easily. The problem more often is one of *how* to join the discussion to make these contributions effectively.

Good participants join the discussion when they have something to say that adds to what has been said and bears directly on the subject. There is very little room at most meetings for anecdotes, reminiscences, play-by-play descriptions, and windy speeches. The participant who indulges in them is immediately tagged as counterproductive. Moreover, any contribution to the meeting presented in any of these forms has little impact. The good participant restrains the urge to make speeches and delivers short, pointed statements that waste no time.

Good participants avoid haggling over small, unimportant details. One manager we know refers to hagglers as "the nitty-gritty people." He says they can be counted on to debate the precise meaning of a single word while the rest of the participants are trying to formulate a paragraph.

Good participants don't interrupt a speaker in the middle of a thought to insert a new idea into the meeting. This is a matter of common courtesy, but it is also a matter of good listening and good meeting strategy. Ideas inserted this way get thrown aside because they demand that the participants switch from one flow of thought to another in midstream.

Good participants always ask questions to clarify their understanding as one means of joining the discussion. If these questions are sharp, succinct, and addressed directly to the topic, everyone in a meeting appreciates them. Good questions directed to the heart of the matter aid everyone's understanding.

The Bottom-Line Technique

There are two ways to express an idea when your turn comes at a meeting—one good and one bad. The good one might be called the "bottom-line method"; the bad one, the "joke method."

The joke technique gets poor reception in meetings. A joke teller carefully builds a story in great detail, working up to a final punch line at the end. The listener never understands the whole idea until that punch line is delivered, and a good joke teller can keep listeners hanging for a long time before getting to the punch line. In a meeting, when the joke technique is used, the other participants listen, waiting for the kernel of the idea—and it never seems to come. When the punch line finally is delivered, impatience has dulled their interest and their reception is likely to be poor. The joke technique takes too much time and reduces the value of the idea being presented.

The bottom-line technique, on the other hand, is always the best way to present an idea. In it, the kernel of the contribution is presented in the first sentence or two, and then elaborated or explained in the following sentences. In this situation, the participants can start thinking about it instantly, and expand the concept as it is explained or clarified. With the bottom-line technique, ideas are brought out quicker and the discussion moves along at a better rate.

A Formula for Presenting Ideas

There is a basic step-by-step formula that is useful in preparing an idea for a meeting.

1. Think the idea through before presenting it. Look for flaws and feel assured that it will work before placing it in the running.

2. Think out a crisp, organized presentation. Plan a few sentences that make the idea understandable, select the major benefits and points that give it value, and if it has weaknesses, indicate them, showing how they are outweighed by the benefits.

3. Be prepared to defend the idea when the discussion starts. Understand its vulnerable points and have answers for possible questions.

4. Lay out not only the idea, but also how it can be implemented. Other participants will visualize the idea much more clearly when they can see it in action.

This method is presented as a formula, but when used regularly it becomes a pattern for thinking habits. Persons trained to think in these logical steps can perform them almost instantly on any idea that is presented. They quickly gain reputations as "clear thinkers." The training consists of no more than always applying these four steps to every problem, in or out of a meeting. As the method becomes a habit, the speed with which it can be performed increases until it becomes known as "thinking on your feet."

Most of us go through a similar mental process before making any kind of a presentation or decision—from planning the dates for a vacation to requesting a raise. However, for some reason, many people don't break the procedure into steps and recognize that it is a process that can be followed when preparing for a meeting or a discussion.

The Politics of Presenting an Idea

Business ideas travel in two directions: from top management down and from lower management up. All too often, the merit in an idea is determined by where it came from rather than whether it is the best idea. This is a fact of business life. When the boss offers an idea, it is enhanced by the stamp of his or her authority and unless it is a patently bad idea, immediately earns top consideration. When an idea wells up from the lower ranks, it comes without the stamp of authority. It must be a sound idea that is carefully presented and able to stand alone and be defended.

This condition suggests that top management, including the meeting leader, should be very careful about presenting ideas at meetings before the participants have had an opportunity to place their suggestions in the running. The idea sent down from the top may carry so much weight that it smothers other, better ideas that might emerge during the meeting.

Participants, on the other hand, must exercise some care in offering new ideas. First, any idea coming up from the lower ranks should be tested beforehand, usually through discussion with your superior. Second, the idea must be very well-developed before its presentation. A partially developed idea can be picked apart quickly and discarded by the group. Third, it must be communicated so that everyone at the table clearly and immediately understands it. And finally, it must be presented at the proper moment during the meeting—usually after all other ideas have been aired and before intense discussion begins.

Two "Don'ts" for Participants

There are two kinds of ideas at a meeting. One is generated and developed during the discussion; the other is brought in whole and offered to the group for approval or further development. Group-generated ideas usually have no author. However, when one person offers an idea, that person is the author, for better or for worse. Inherent in the idea of authorship is the thought that if the idea is successful, the author gets the credit.

Don't take credit for ideas that aren't yours. Suppose that at an earlier meeting an idea was offered by someone. Now another participant takes the idea, expands and refines it, and presents it as his or her own contribution—much to the displeasure of the person who initiated the idea in the first place and others around the table who remember how the idea started.

Improving an earlier idea in itself is good but taking credit for the original idea is not. The wise thing is to give immediate credit for the source. It can be done in an easy sentence, such as, "Margaret gave us an idea last week that has merit." Margaret's idea is then briefly outlined before an improved or amended version is offered. In this way, the credit can be shared gracefully.

Don't openly damn other ideas. Very often, when offering an idea, a participant may be bucking another idea which was presented earlier. The wrong way to introduce a new idea in these circumstances is to say, "I think Jerry's idea is terrible. I have a better one." The obvious better way is to say, "Jerry's idea has many good points and is one way to handle the situation. I'd like to suggest an alternate course that we might consider."

Take Home Personal Minutes

Meeting leaders are advised to prepare minutes after a meeting, and to distribute copies of them within a day or so of the meeting. They may or may not do this. For this reason if no other, wise participants keep a set of notes on their agenda sheets to take back to their own offices. These can be filed for later reference. The notes should show the major points that came up in discussion, what determinations were made, and what work assignments were handed out.

Summary

The good participant knows how to listen, how to join a discussion, how to make a contribution, how to join with others in arriving at a clear-cut decision—and how to disagree constructively.

There are three good reasons to be an active participant in company meetings: (1) to contribute to the success of the company, (2) by contribution to the company, to gain recognition and eventual promotion, and (3) by active participation, to learn more about good meetings and about the company itself.

The Rules of Good Listening

The first skill a participant needs is the ability to listen. Two common listening flaws are inattention and mentally racing ahead of the meeting. Good listening can be developed into a habit through constant practice. The greatest barrier to good listening is inattentiveness. The rules for good listening are:

1. Establish frequent eye contact with the meeting leader or speaking participants.
2. Always hear the ideas—not the words—being presented.
3. Block out thoughts that aren't a part of the meeting.
4. Work at increasing your attention span.
5. Take notes of key words during a discussion to keep your attention focused on the meeting.
6. Ignore a speaker's faulty delivery or lapses in logic.

How to Prepare an Idea for Presentation

1. Think the idea through and feel sure it will work before presenting it.
2. Think out an organized presentation of the major benefits. Indicate weaknesses, but show how they are outweighed by the benefits.
3. Be prepared to defend the idea. Know where it may be attacked and have answers for possible questions.
4. Show how the idea can be implemented.

How to Join a Discussion

1. Good participants join a discussion when they have something to say that adds to what has been said and bears directly on the subject.

There is no room at meetings for anecdotes, reminiscences, play-by-play descriptions, and windy speeches.

2. Good participants avoid haggling over small, unimportant details.

3. Good participants don't interrupt a speaker in the middle of a thought to insert a new idea into the meeting.

4. Good participants always ask questions to clarify their understanding as one means of joining the discussion.

The Bottom-Line Technique

The bottom-line technique is the best way to present an idea in a discussion. The kernel of the contribution is presented in the first sentence or two, then elaborated or explained in the following sentences.

The joke technique, in which the listeners are held in suspense while the presenter builds to a climactic punch line, gets poor reception in meetings. The audience loses interest, and the presentation takes too long, reducing the value of the idea.

8

The Wharton Study and Beyond

In 1981, 3M asked the Wharton Applied Research Center of the University of Pennsylvania to conduct a study on the effects of overhead visuals on business meetings. And, in 1985, 3M supported research at the University of Minnesota concerning the effectiveness of computer-generated graphics in the meeting setting.

While we felt strongly about the use of visuals and had observed firsthand how they improve meetings, our feelings constituted nothing more than a good body of anecdotal evidence, and there was no current laboratory research to support them. Anecdotal evidence must be backed by controlled studies in which sound, repeatable data are developed. We, of course, were not the only people with feelings about the use of good visuals. Most serious students of the meeting felt the same way, which is why the use of visuals had increased over the years. However a serious study of the effect of visuals in a meeting was needed.

It was for this reason that we approached the Wharton Research Center initially and the University of Minnesota several years later. The goal of these studies was to determine, under stringent scientific conditions, if there was a correlation between the use of visuals in a meeting and the eventual effectiveness of that meeting.

During preliminary discussions, researchers at both institutions made it clear that we were funding research, not results, and that, while we believed the use of visuals increased the effectiveness and productivity of business meetings, there was no assurance that a study could produce meaningful, measurable results to corroborate our feelings. There was, in fact, the possibility that our observations might be shown to have no significance. However, the need for serious studies was apparent, and we determined to fund them regardless of the outcome.

The Business Meeting Background

On the surface, a business meeting is a simple device: a group of men and women get together in a room to discuss a business-related subject. Their pooled knowledge and experience is brought to bear on problems and to create plans. Knowledge and information are passed along through meetings. There seems to be nothing complicated about the business meeting process. But our experience has shown that business meetings are a long way from being that simple, and that they have been abused and misused to the extent that they have earned a terrible reputation as costly time wasters—and as the bane of the executive's existence.

Considering the fact that businesses can't be run without meetings, and that one of the marks of an efficient, successful, growing company is the quality of its meetings, the bad reputation of meetings has always seemed to be an anomaly. Recognizing that meetings cannot be eliminated, we believe that the only possible answer has been to improve them.

Meetings built around visuals always seemed better to us. When we compared similar meetings, those in which visuals were employed were more productive. The participants seemed more interested and involved; the presenters seemed better prepared; and the meetings seemed to move faster, with fewer breakdowns and less wasted time.

The Wharton Study

The independent scientific study carried out at the Wharton Applied Research Center at the Wharton School of the University of Pennsylvania was called, "A Study of the Effects of the Use of Overhead Transparencies on Business Meetings." It was designed specifically to answer the following questions:

1. Does the use of overhead transparencies in a business meeting presentation affect either the individual decisions made or the final group decision?

2. Does the use of overhead transparencies in a business meeting presentation affect participants' perceptions of the presenters?

3. Does the use of overhead transparencies in a business meeting have an effect on particular characteristics of meetings, perceived effectiveness or efficiency, or interaction patterns of the participants?

To assess these effects, business meetings at Wharton were simulated under controlled conditions. Participants were informed that they were meeting to make a decision about the introduction of a new product. Background information relevant to the decision was provided in a case-history format. Two presenters argued for and against the introduction of the product. The participants had the opportunity to ask questions of the presenters, to discuss the matter among themselves, and to attempt to reach a consensus about the appropriate decision.

The participants were MBA students from the Wharton School and Drexel University who had prior exposure to marketing cases and/or business experience. The study consisted of a total sample of 36 groups and 123 subjects, with each group consisting of either three or four subjects.

Three experimental conditions were set up. In one, the pro presenter used overhead transparencies while the con presenter did not. In another, these roles were reversed, with the con presenter using the overhead transparencies. In a third setting, neither presenter used overhead transparencies. When presenters did not use overhead transparencies, they used a whiteboard to emphasize their points. Twelve groups were exposed to each of these conditions. In each group session, the participants were videotaped and the tapes were studied later.

The Wharton Study Findings

Some very important findings came out of the study (Figures 8.1 to 8.4). They clearly show that visuals—specifically overhead transparencies—in a business meeting make major differences. Coupled with our own experience, they lead us to recommend that visuals be used as a part of all meetings when possible. The major findings are as follows.

> Overhead transparencies had an impact on meeting outcome, perceptions of the presenter and meeting process.*

Presenters using overhead transparencies were "perceived as signifi-

---

*From the Wharton Study, the Wharton Research Center, University of Pennsylvania.

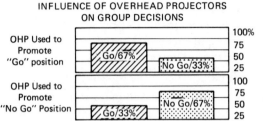

INFLUENCE OF OVERHEAD PROJECTORS
ON GROUP DECISIONS

Figure 8.1

cantly better prepared, more professional, more persuasive, more highly credible and more interesting."

Group decisions were reached faster and meetings were shorter when overhead transparencies were used.

More favorable responses to their business propositions concerning the introduction of the new product (either pro or con) were won by presenters using overhead transparencies.

Less time was spent on lengthy monologues, while verbal exchanges were increased. According to the study, "Communication experts generally believe that the less time spent in monologue, the more efficient the meeting, because more real interaction of ideas is allowed to take place."

Meetings were shorter when overhead transparencies were used. With the use of transparencies, the median duration of the group sessions was 18.6 minutes. Without the use of transparencies, the median duration was 25.75 minutes. Thus the use of overhead projectors reduced the average length of meetings by 28 percent.

> . . . the use of overhead transparencies can have an influence on the actual decision reached, both on an individual and group level.*

Decisions by the participants were called for at three points: immediately after the presentation; after group discussion; and after the group had reached its decision. At each point, the decision favored the presenter who used the overhead projector. As the chart indicates, this presenter (representing either the pro or the con side) won 66 percent of the time at decision point 1, 72 percent of the time at decision point 2, and 65 percent of the time at decision point 3.

---

*From the Wharton Study, the Wharton Research Center, University of Pennsylvania.

Although the study doesn't go into why overhead projection visuals increased the chance for a decision in favor of the presenter, we believe several factors are responsible. First, the visuals support the presenter's throughts and words. It is estimated that we retain only 10 percent of what we hear, but when visuals are added, the retention rate increases to 50 percent. Thus, more of what the presenter says is remembered when the time comes for a decision—and probably less of what is said is misunderstood or misconstrued. Second, we feel that the preparation of overhead transparencies forces the presenter to organize and crystallize his or her thoughts more concisely before the meeting. This produces a better, more easily absorbed presentation, and leads to faster, more productive meetings. There may be a less obvious, more subtle reason. Presenters exhibit organization and control throughout the presentation with overhead transparencies. This tends to convey the idea that they know what they're doing. They become more convincing, more persuasive, and more influential.

The discussion in groups where overhead transparencies were used in-

INFLUENCE OF OVERHEAD
PROJECTOR USAGE ON
MEETING OUTCOME

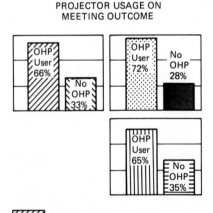

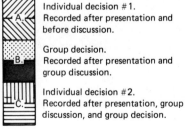

Individual decision #1.
Recorded after presentation and
before discussion.

Group decision.
Recorded after presentation and
group discussion.

Individual decision #2.
Recorded after presentation, group
discussion, and group decision.

Figure 8.2

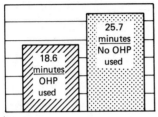

INFLUENCE OF OVERHEAD
PROJECTOR USAGE ON
AVERAGE MEETING LENGTH

Results

Use of overhead projectors
reduced average length
of meetings by 28%.

Figure 8.3

cluded less time in long restatements of position and more time in active interaction than when overhead transparencies were not used.*

When groups interact more, they understand more. Interactive discussion broadens the understanding of all participants as meanings and nuances are explored, new ideas and interpretations offered, and reasoning by individuals explained. Without interaction, ideas remain fixed and limited to individual experience. In every effective meeting, the meeting leader strives to develop interactive discussion, hoping to draw on the experience and brain power around the table. The less the interactive discussion, the less this precious resource is utilized.

> Groups in which one of the presenters used overhead transparencies were more likely to reach a consensus on their decision than groups where no overhead transparencies were used.*

The report found that groups exposed to overhead presentations were more likely to reach a firm, fast, favorable decision. The report states that "individual participants reported making their decisions earlier when overhead transparencies were used than when they were not."

This suggests important implications: the participants may have felt more decisive because they had a better command of the facts resulting from the visual presentation. Clearly, their decisions favored the side of the discussion presented orally and visually, not just orally. Though the study does not say so, we believe they "favored" the side represented by

---

*From the Wharton Study, the Wharton Research Center, University of Pennsylvania.

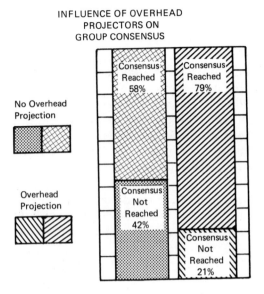

INFLUENCE OF OVERHEAD
PROJECTORS ON
GROUP CONSENSUS

Figure 8.4

visuals because they felt they had a better understanding of the points involved.

> Consensus was reached in 79 percent of the groups which were exposed to the use of overhead transparencies, while only 58 percent of the groups who did not view transparencies reached consensus.*

One goal for each group in the study was to attempt to arrive at a decision by consensus within the time allotted. Researchers reported that there was a statistically significant difference between the number of groups reaching a consensus when transparencies were used compared to those groups in which transparencies were not used. Better than 24 percent more meetings were successful in achieving their stated goals after the participants had seen visual presentations.

> The presenter who used overhead transparencies in his presentation was perceived as significantly better prepared, more professional, more persuasive, more credible and more interesting than the presenter who did not use overhead transparencies.*

The success of any meeting depends to a large extent on the quality of presentations. A critical aspect is the way the presentation is perceived by

---

*From the Wharton Study, the Wharton Research Center, University of Pennsylvania.

those attending the meeting. The work of the meeting is much more likely to be accomplished quickly and successfully when the participants see the presenter as professional, prepared, and credible. The implications for beginning and younger managers in this finding are important since to a large extent, their careers hinge on how they are perceived by their peers and superiors in action at meetings.

The Wharton Study clearly shows the impact of overhead visuals in a business presentation, leaving little doubt that when the meeting situation permits it, such presentations should be used. This, we believe, should include meetings that frequently are considered "too small" to require a visual presentation. Any meeting can be built around a few easy-to-make visuals. In the following chapters, we will look into the different types of visual presentations and how to design and prepare presentations. It should be noted that the Wharton study specifically dealt with the use of overhead transparencies in visual presentations. Other types of visuals, such as 35-mm slides, charts, videotaped programs, etc., were not covered and the findings of the study should not be used to include them.

The University of Minnesota/ 3M Study

Although a full evaluation of the University of Minnesota/3M Study of computer graphics had not been completed when the final touches were being put on this book, several major findings had surfaced.

The first of these is that presentations using visual aids (overhead transparencies and 35-mm slides) were 43 percent more persuasive than unaided presentations.

The study also found that presenters using computer-generated visuals were perceived as being:

- More concise
- More professional
- Clearer
- More persuasive
- More interesting
- More effective in the use of supporting data

Audience reaction in terms of attention, comprehension, agreement, and retention was also found to be better when presentation support was used than when it was not.

The University of Minnesota/3M study went further in some respects than did the Wharton Study. Color, for example, was found to be significantly more persuasive than black and white in the design of presentation support. And, as a means of enciting meeting participants to action, color overhead transparencies seemed to have the greatest impact.

But researchers at the Management Information Research Center who conducted the study also warned that technological capability greatly exceeds current levels of user understanding of the effective applications of computer graphics. For this reason, use of image-enhanced graphics—those with substantial amounts of pictorial material—was recommended only for specific purposes:

- To increase information density
- To display multiple dimensions
- To organize complex issues
- To support abstract concepts
- To illustrate trends

The study cautioned computer graphics users to utilize image-enhanced graphics selectively and carefully in order to avoid confusing rather than enlightening an audience.

"When in doubt," the study concludes, "use plain text."

Another interesting observation. Neither the use of overhead transparencies nor the use of 35-mm slides was found to be a superior method of persuasion. Audiences, however, did perceive them differently. Slides were found to heighten peceptions of professionalism. Overhead transparencies seemed to make a presenter more interesting.

Summary

The Wharton Study found that when overhead visuals were used in business meetings, they resulted in:

1. Shorter meetings.
2. Faster group decisions.
3. Perception of presenter as more professional, better prepared.
4. Greater perception of the subject by participants.
5. Less wasted discussion time in the meeting.
6. More meetings successfully arriving at decisions.

Specific Findings

1. Overhead transparencies had an impact on meeting outcome, perceptions of the presenter, and meeting process. Presenters using

overhead transparencies were "perceived as significantly better prepared, more professional, more persuasive, more highly credible, and
more interesting."

2. Group decisions were reached faster and meetings completed their
work faster when overhead transparencies were used. Groups in which
one of the presenters used overhead transparencies were more likely to
reach a consensus on their decision than groups where no overhead
transparencies were used.

3. More favorable responses to their business propositions concerning the introduction of the new product (either pro or con) were won by
presenters using overhead transparencies.

4. Less time was spent on lengthy monologues, while verbal exchanges
increased. Discussion in groups where overhead transparencies were
used took up less time in long restatements of position and more time in
active interaction than when overhead tranparencies were not used.

5. Meetings were shorter when overhead transparencies were used.
With transparencies, the median duration of the group sessions was 18.6
minutes. Without transparencies, the median duration was 25.75 minutes. Thus the use of overhead projectors reduced the average length of
meetings by 28 percent.

6. The use of overhead transparencies can have an influence on the
actual decision reached, on both an individual and a group level.

Although all the implications of the University of Minnesota/3M Study
had not been explored before this book went to press, the findings
generally supported the earlier Wharton Study and added some new
dimensions:

1. Presentations using visual aids (overhead transparencies and 35-
mm slides) were 43 percent more persuasive than unaided presentations.

2. Color was found to be significantly more persuasive than black and
white in the design of presentation support.

3. Neither the use of overhead transparencies nor the use of 35-mm
slides was found to be a superior method of persuasion. But slides were
found to heighten an audience's perception of professionalism; overhead transparencies seemed to make a presenter more interesting.

9
Visual Presentation Methods

Tom Hope, of Hope Reports, Inc., a leading consultant and market research expert in the audiovisual field, provides data that show the current growth of the use of visuals in business meetings. In 1985, over $4.5 billion was spent in the United States to produce more than 500 million original 35-mm slides for professional use. He anticipates that by 1990, the annual production may reach 750 million original slides, representing an investment of $10 billion a year. These figures do not include the consumer slide market.

Overhead transparencies have witnessed a similar growth in recent years. Hope says, "In 1985, in excess of 400 million overhead transparencies were used and they are experiencing the same kind of growth as 35 mm slides. The great majority of overhead transparencies are made on office copiers in the users' offices, not done by professionals.

"Overhead projectors were introduced in 1945 and immediately adopted by educators. Overhead use in schools reached a peak in 1966, after which there was a dropoff. But the development of the portable overhead projector kindled a renaissance and business discovered overheads for meeting use about that time. The use of overheads has climbed steadily for more than ten years.

"During the rest of this decade we see an explosive increase in the use of computer graphics for developing visuals taking place. In 1985, seven percent of all slides were computer generated and by 1990, the number may exceed 20 percent. These figures include slides ordered through computer graphic services, from a local supplier, or made by users on their own equipment. In addition, we are seeing a new use of the office microcomputer—the growing use of presentation graphic materials for small meetings generated right on the desktop CRT, without the need for slides.

"This growth in all forms of presentation visuals," Hope concludes, "is taking place because business people have recognized the impact value they offer. People can grasp the significance of a graph much quicker than when they see a lot of numbers, and visualization adds a colorful, dramatic touch to figures which otherwise might be very dull."

Graphics Simplify and Clarify

The increasing complexity of business and the enormous volume of information generated by computers have made it necessary to turn to graphics to simplify and clarify information. One chart or graph may succinctly sum up the essence of a multipage report. Dr. Marshall Hatfield, vice president of 3M's Audio-Visual Division, says, "I recall a case in which the use of computer-generated graphics enabled a corporation to reduce a monthly 100-page report to one sheet of graphs. The result was an immense saving of time and increased productivity."

The need to simplify and clarify data is an obvious reason for the use of visuals. The Wharton Study has provided some strong underlying reasons that were not obvious until the study brought them out. The study revealed that overhead visuals produced quicker decisions, and that presenters who used them were more apt to win favorable decisions. Topping all of this was the fact that presentations using overhead transparencies resulted in meetings that were on average 28 percent shorter—once again an increase in meeting efficiency.

Most meetings deal with facts in a three-step procedure: presentation of the facts—followed by an interpretation of the facts—followed by an application of the facts as interpreted. Obviously, the clearer the presentation of the facts, the quicker and better the interpretation and application will be.

When Visuals Are Needed

Visuals become absolutely necessary when a meeting group is faced with assimilating masses of data; sales, cost, and other forecasts or results;

financial information; technical material and drawings; etc. They are less necessary in meetings involving discussion of policies and similar subjects, but even in these meetings, headline and summary visuals keep the group alert and on its agenda. Once used principally in large-scale meetings, visual presentations are now being extended to typical daily meetings previously thought too small to merit graphics. Executives and managers have discovered the power of graphic presentations to increase meeting productivity at every level of company business.

In addition to their power to increase meeting efficiency, visual presentations have spread to daily "regular" meetings because new technologies have made available a variety of low-cost, easy-to-operate equipment to project quality 35-mm slides and overhead transparencies, and also provided the means of creating slides and transparencies for this equipment quickly and at low cost.

Types of Presentations

Visuals can be brought to a meeting in a number of ways, from flip charts and easel pads to 35-mm slides and overhead transparencies to videotaped presentations on a TV monitor. The choice of a medium may be a matter of what is available; what is most effective for the subject matter, the room and the size of the audience; and what suits the style of the presenter best.

Tom Hope likes to compare making presentations to a game of golf. "You don't play with a single golf club," he says. "You have a whole collection, from drivers to putters, to meet every circumstance you might encounter. It's the same with presentation media. You don't try to do everything with slides or overheads. You find the best medium for each situation."

This chapter looks at the basic types of presentation media and offers pointers on how to select and use the right one for each situation. Later, we will present a short course in the design and production of effective visuals for different situations and investigate the whole question of how to—and how not to—design charts and graphs.

Presenting You, the Individual

Every presentation has four elements: the words, the visuals, the equipment, and *you*, the presenter. You are not just a machine for delivering the presentation nor are you simply the operator of the slide or overhead equipment. You are the center of the presentation. Its success depends on the way the audience perceives you in relation to the presentation. They must have respect for you, believe you, relate to you, rely on you. The words and the visuals really mean much less without the "you" factor. We point this out because we feel that a major consideration in the selection of a presentation medium is the opportunity it provides the presenter to relate to the audience.

Learning to Use the Equipment

The actual operation of an overhead or a slide projector is easy, and a polished style of presentation isn't hard to develop. All of us who make meeting presentations need to take the time to become practiced in the use of the equipment we expect to use. Presenters who stumble through a presentation, unable to smoothly move from one graphic to another, distract the audience and reduce the effectiveness of the presentation. A little practice makes it possible not only to make a smooth professional presentation but also to use the special techniques the equipment offers. In the case of overhead projectors this includes revelations, overlays, and write-ons; with 35-mm slide projectors, it includes successive slides to create builds and revelations.

The goal of a presenter should be to make the operation of the equipment so easy and natural that the audience is unaware of it.

Modern Methods of Presentation

The television-oriented audiences of today are accustomed to powerful, professionally produced visual presentations. Any major presentation which doesn't take advantage of modern visual vehicles risks drawing a negative result. Some of the older methods, such as flip charts, can still be used effectively under some specialized circumstances so we will talk about them, but most business meeting presentations should use the most modern method available.

The following is a brief description of some types of equipment used today in making graphic presentations.

The Chalkboard

The chalkboard, dating back to school days, is probably the simplest, easiest-to-use, and least expensive of visual communications devices. When presenters turn to the board to print out statements as they talk, they bring a sense of spontaneity to the presentation. In some situations, such as the scientific lecture or a development discussion between engineers, the chalkboard may be the best method. However, in more general business meetings, it has limitations that can cause a loss of audience attention. Presenters must turn their backs to the audience as they write on the board, diminishing the "you" factor. Hand printing more than a word or two takes time and interrupts the flow of the presentation. Printing legibly at high speed is difficult for most people. The chalk can break or squeak. When the board is full, the presenter must find the eraser and rub it across the board while he or she keeps talking. This can be distracting.

Easel Pad Presentations

An easel pad is an oversized pad of paper mounted on an easel at the front of the meeting room. The speaker writes on it with black or colored felt-tipped markers or grease pencils. It has the same advantage of spontaneity and the same disadvantages of the chalkboard—presenters turning their backs to the audience, interrupted speech flow, and illegible printing. A major advantage is that erasing isn't necessary. When the top page on the pad is full, it is flipped back to reveal a clean, new page. Because of their size, both chalkboards and easel pads must be limited to use before small groups, but can be effective under the right circumstances.

Chart Presentations

Presentations built around prepared charts have been popular for a long time. The charts, on large artboards, are displayed on an easel at the front of the room, and the presenter removes each chart to expose the next one as the presentation proceeds. The charts can be elaborately finished or may just be rough finals—both work well. Prepared chart presentations of this type, however, are giving way to overhead projector transparencies and 35-mm slides, in which the same charts can be projected. Charts work particularly well in overhead projector presentations, where they are easily handled by the presenter, quick and inexpensive to make, and provide tremendous flexibility in modes of presentation. With the advent of computer-generated 35-mm color slides, beautiful charts of professional quality can be designed, ordered, and delivered in less than 2 days. Either the slide or the transparency is an ideal modern substitute for the standard chart presentation.

Overhead Projection

In overhead projection, a transparency is placed on the horizontal "stage" of the projector and the image is projected to a white matte (dull-finish) screen mounted on a wall or stand. The advantages of this method have given it wide acceptance in business and education. Some of the major benefits are:

1. The presentation can be made in a fully lighted room.
2. The presenter faces the audience for eye contact and interaction.
3. The projector is placed at the front of the room beside the speaker, who has complete control and can operate it without assistance as the presentation proceeds.
4. It permits interesting display techniques such as revelation, in which one line at a time on a visual is revealed to the audience; the overlay, in which a graphic is built up by placing one transparency over another; and the write-on technique, where the presenter writes directly on the surface of a transparency as it is projected. With these techniques it is easy, for example, to heighten interest in a 5-year financial chart by adding the figures year by year and then circling significant figures on the chart.
5. Overhead transparencies are easily made and don't require long processing time. Any document can be converted into a transparency in seconds on a plain-paper copier or infrared transparency maker.
6. Overhead projectors are silent.
7. A presenter can easily operate two projectors focused on two screens, allowing dramatic movement and presentation development.

The overhead projector provides spontaneity and personal involvement by presenters, who can write on a blank transparency sheet with a felt-tipped marker and have the words appear on the screen as they write. For emphasis, presenters can circle or underline items on a chart or key words. By overlaying one transparency on another, they can build a story right on the screen—for instance, adding sales results year by year to build a complete report.

All things considered, the overhead projector offers the most flexible method of presenting visuals to audiences of small to moderate size. With the portable units now available, the overhead works well in small office meetings.

35-mm Slide Presentations

Presentations consisting of projected 35-mm slides can be colorful and exciting, and are particularly good for use in front of large audiences. In theater settings, slides can be projected to 8 by 8 feet or larger. Progressive buildup of a visual can be achieved by projecting a series of slides. The use of several synchronized projectors can produce a fast-paced show that has much of the drama of a motion picture production at a lower cost. Many of the old problems of producing high-quality slides and transparencies have been eliminated by computer-generated slide services. Now professional-quality slides no longer take weeks to produce but can be ordered by phone and be ready in a few days.

Good-quality slides allow projection in rooms with the lighting only dimmed. This makes it a little less easy to take notes and for the presenter to see the audience. However, the power and impact of strong, colorful slides makes this type of presentation extremely valuable in spite of these minor drawbacks. Slide presentations tend to be somewhat more impersonal than those with an overhead projector.

Videotape Presentations

According to Tom Hope, the use of video in meetings continues to increase and videodisc use, though the volume is still small, is up dramatically.

Videotaped programs are replacing motion picture use in smaller business meetings. They are easy to handle during a meeting, since no threading of the film through the projector is needed. The videocassette is simply inserted into the videotape player. Videotaped programs offer advantages similar to motion pictures—integration of theme, sight, sound, color, and motion. If copies of the presentation are needed, the video program can be easily duplicated.

Video presentations are limited to use before small audiences because of the small size of video monitors commonly available. Video projectors which deliver pictures up to 8 feet in diagonal measurement can be used for larger meetings, but images on these big screens are weaker and have less definition than either smaller TV sets or 16-mm motion pictures. Also, they tend to wash out in bright room light, so projected presentations must be viewed in dimly lighted rooms. Technology in this area is advancing, and sharper, brighter pictures in the future will overcome this drawback.

To achieve professional quality in major videotaped presentations, professional editing and production assistance is necessary. Otherwise the presentation may have that "home movie" look, which is acceptable for quick in-house productions but not for dressy presentations before sophisticated modern audiences. Such audiences expect a professional production when they look at a monitor and tend to be intolerant of home movie productions.

Once a videotaped presentation is finished, last-minute editing isn't practical so presentations using videotaped segments must be planned well in advance to allow for production and editing.

Motion Picture Presentations

After videotape programs came into use, it appeared that they would replace motion pictures for corporate programming. However, rising costs in the editing of videotaped productions have altered that projection. More producers are going back to motion picture film for the filming and editing of the original production. As a result, according to Tom Hope, contract film production done by independent film producers in the U.S., after an initial falloff, has returned to popularity with an 11 percent increase in 1984 and continued increases since then. At the same time, the use of videotape for original productions was down 1 percent from previous levels. However, once a program has been produced, the videotape format is easier to distribute and use, so many film productions are now duplicated on videotape.

Original presentations in either film or videotape require scripting, filming, and complicated postproduction; thus they are expensive to produce. However, for very large meetings, or where the cost can be amortized by showings at a number of meetings, these presentations can be very effective. For example, in a sales presentation to a new client, the inclusion of a short film clip on the history of the company or of an innovative manufacturing process adds a very professional touch and undoubtedly says more than words alone could possibly convey. Such clips can be used many times, making their production cost-effective.

Multimedia Presentations

The full-blown "dog and pony" show—that extravaganza usually reserved for the annual motivation of the national sales force or for major new product introductions—can be a combination of any or all of the presentation methods mentioned, plus the addition of a live stage show and a full orchestra. The automobile industry favors this way of introducing new models.

Something less than this full-blown, Las Vegas–style presentation can be put together by combining 35-mm slides and videotape or motion pictures into a basic presentation built around an overhead projector. Any number of visual combinations can be worked out that make a fast-paced, impressive multimedia show. The larger and more complicated the show, the more the need for professional help in the production itself and in the operation of the equipment. Multiprojector slide shows using as many as 40 projectors on multiple screens have been developed, though the average number of projectors for multiprojector shows now is about nine.

Even in smaller multimedia productions, the presenter must have technicians to operate the equipment, and many timed rehearsals are necessary to achieve a final smooth coordination.

Choosing the Best Presentation Method

Which is the best method to use in a presentation? That depends on the type and purpose of the presentation, the presenter, the size of the audience, and the place where the presentation will be made. It also depends to a large extent on personal preferences. Not all visual aids are well-suited to the typical business meeting environment. Motion pictures and videotapes require long lead times for preparation and can be quite expensive. They are best reserved for big meetings with ample planning time, or meetings where special flash and pizzazz is wanted and where multimedia presentations work well. Flip chart and chalkboard presentations are best used before groups of 10 or less, and generally contribute best in technical discussions.

Chalkboards and easel pads, while easy to use and somewhat spontaneous, are highly restrictive. They depend on the presenter's ability to talk and print legibly at the same time, and work best before small, closely integrated audiences. Presentations using prepared charts work well but can be expensive to produce and may require long lead time and professional help to prepare.

Anything that can be done with other visual media can also be done with overhead transparencies or 35-mm slides. They are easy to use, offer the advantages of color, and offer the presenter full control through the use of the various reveal, overlay, and sequence-building techniques.

With overhead projection, a presentation can be made to a group of any size in a fully lighted room. The presenter faces the audience, has better meeting control, and is able to pick up group reactions immediately. If necessary, a presenter can edit and make on-the-spot changes as the presentation is being assembled. Overhead transparencies are quick and inexpensive to make on either a plain-paper copier or infrared transparency maker. Or they can be computer-generated, ordered by phone, and be ready in a few days.

For the average smaller business meeting, the overhead projection method probably has the greater number of advantages. Its flexibility and the opportunity for personal involvement by the presenter is superior to other techniques.

Slides are best for presentations to medium- and larger-sized audiences in big rooms. Because the room lighting must be dimmed, group participation is not as good, but audience attention and impact is heightened. Computer-generated slide services have brought the cost, turnaround time, and accessibility of effective 35-mm slides more in line with that of overhead transparencies.

Setting Up the Room for Visuals

No matter how good the graphics, the presentation won't work unless the audience can see it without difficulty. The meeting room should be set up to make the most of the visual equipment and materials to be used. Here are guidelines on the placement of screens and projectors, orientation of the room, and screen size that permit the most effective visual presentations (Figures 9.1 to 9.3).

1. For slide and film presentations, place the screen in a front corner of the room to permit a clear view by the entire audience. The presenter can be at a podium in the front center of the room. If the screen is placed in the center of the stage and the presenter moved to one side, the emphasis switches from the presenter to the graphics. Generally, the emphasis should stay on the presenter, with the graphic presentation used to reinforce what he or she has to say.

2. For overhead projector presentations, place the screen at an angle in the left-hand corner of the room, with the presenter located at the right center (as you look from the back of the room). Presenters stand beside the projector facing the audience, which allows them to stay in contact with the group while changing transparencies or writing on the projector stage.

3. Matte-finish screens must be used because of the sharp angles at which the audience views the screen. Our tests show that a matte-finish

screen provides up to 130° of visibility. Beaded or lenticular screens will perform poorly at these angles. See the accompanying visibility chart.

4. The screens must be tilted forward at the top (or back at the bottom) to prevent image "keystoning," a distortion of the image in which the top is wider than the bottom. To eliminate keystoning, the top of the screen must be the same distance from the projector lens as the bottom of the screen—and the screen is tilted to achieve this.

Tripod screens can be purchased with an accessory known as a "keystone eliminator" to accommodate vertical screen angle.

5. Permanently mounted screens should be located far enough from the wall to permit antikeystone tilting.

6. Presenters should be located at one end of the meeting room's narrow dimension to save space. If the screen is placed midway along the

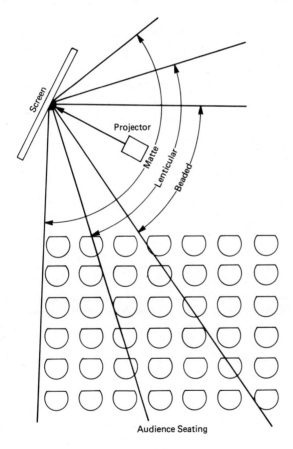

Figure 9.1 Maximum image reflection.

Screen Size

Screen size must be equated to distance between screen and person sitting farthest from the screen. Screen size dictates magnification possible from projector to screen.

Farthest Distance to Screen	20'	25'	30'	35'	40'	45'	50'
Screen Size	50" × 50"	60" × 60"	70" × 70"	84" × 84"	96" × 96"	9' × 9'	10' × 10'

Room Size vs. Ceiling Height

Distance from Front to Rear	0'–30'	30'–40'	40'–50'	50'–60'	Over 60'
Ceiling Height	9'	10'	11'	12'	Over 12'

Projector to Screen Distances

Standard overhead projectors such as those sold by 3M Company are manufactured with a 14-inch focal length projection lens.

Projector to screen distance depends upon screen size; the larger the screen, the greater distance required.

For 14-Inch Focal Length Projectors (with 10.5-inch Stage Aperture)

Projector to Screen Distance	80" (6.5')	94" (7.8')	107" (8.9')	126" (10.5')	142" (11.8')	158" (13.1')	174" (14.5')
Screen Size	50" × 50"	60" × 60"	70" × 70"	84" × 84"	96" × 96"	9' × 9'	10' × 10'

For 10.8-Inch Focal Length Projectors (with 10-inch Stage Aperture)

Projector to Screen Distance	63"	73"	84"	99"	111"
Screen Size	50' × 50'	60' × 60'	70' × 70'	84' × 84'	96' × 96'

Screen Size vs. Projector Distance for Filmstrip, 35-mm Slide Projectors (with 5-inch Focal Length Lens)

Projector to Screen Distance	13'	16'	19'	22'	25'
Screen Size	40" × 40"	50" × 50"	60" × 60"	70" × 70"	80" × 80"

Figure 9.2

long wall, the audience at either end of the room may have difficulty in viewing the screen.

7. The best distance from the screen to the last row in the audience, projector-to-screen distance, etc., for different screen sizes is shown in the table on page 128.

8. Overhead lights should not shine directly on the projection screen. Lights above the screen should be controllable and dimmed during the presentation.

9. Screens for slide and motion picture presentations should be about twice as far from their projectors as screens from overhead projectors. Movie and slide projectors can be used from the rear of the room by changing the angle of the screen.

10. Low ceilings and chandeliers are always a problem in visual

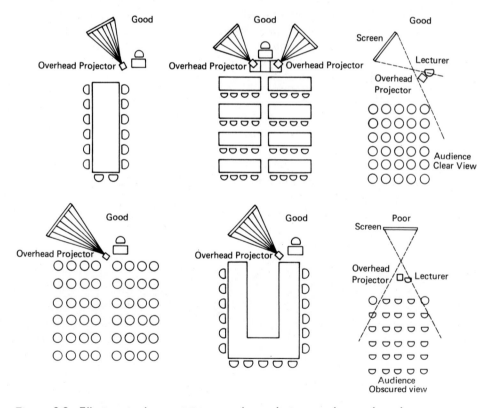

Figure 9.3 Effective visual presentations may be made in any of a number of room configurations. To avoid obscuring the view for some of the audience, place podium and projector to one side, and do not put the screen in the center of the room. As seen in Figure 9.1, a matte screen will provide complete coverage of a room if set off to the side at an angle to the audience.

presentations before a large audience. Avoid them when possible. They limit screen size and the height at which you can mount the screen.

11. Electric outlets should be installed at least every 6 feet in a conference room. When going into a room you've never seen before, check the outlets immediately. Presentation plans may be altered by the availability of convenient outlets—or by the availability of extension cables long enough to reach the outlets.

Summary

Visuals can be brought to a meeting in a number of different ways. The choice of a medium may be a matter of what is available; what is most effective for the subject matter, the room, and the size of the audience; and what best suits the style of the presenter. Today's audiences are accustomed to powerful, professionally produced visual presentations. Any major presentation must take advantage of modern visual vehicles or risk drawing a negative response. Common media available, including older methods, include:

1. The chalkboard
2. The easel pad
3. Prepared charts
4. Overhead projection
5. 35-mm slide projection
6. Videotaped presentations
7. Motion pictures
8. Multimedia presentations

10

How to Design
Good Visuals

Nearly everyone has been exposed to the "memo syndrome" in a meeting. The presenter flashes a whole typewritten memo or letter on the screen while he or she says, "As you can see from this memo, our plans . . . etc." The fact is, you can't see it at all. What you *can* see is 25 lines of typewritten copy too small to read. Or if by chance the type is large enough to read, you need 10 minutes to do it and by that time the presenter has offered a second or third memo for your perusal. Group attention to and participation in presentations like this are, to say the least, minimal.

When we speak of visual presentations, this is not the kind we have in mind. The purpose of this chapter is to lead you to the creation of good graphics.

People think in graphic images and respond to strong graphic presentations, which is why information, and especially masses of figures, should be put into visualized form whenever possible. But the graphics must be designed to *enhance* the presentation and give it impact. They must be attractive, easy to read, and very clear in the statements they make.

The first step in the development of visuals for any presentation is the preparation of a script. The graphics themselves grow out of this script.

How to Generate a Presentation Script

Always develop a working script for any presentation. This is not necessarily a script to be read as a part of the presentation. Hopefully, you will know the material so well you won't have to read it. Rather, this is a script with two main functions: (1) to get all topics to be covered down on paper and (2) to serve as a guide in determining just what visuals or graphics must be developed. It is actually a planning device.

The script allows you to evaluate and prioritize the points to be made in the meeting. Where should the presentation open? What follows logically from the opening? How much time should be allowed for each topic? The application of a little imagination, with your audience firmly in mind, helps align the topics so they make a logical, interesting, and understandable story. For a short presentation, the working script might consist of eight or ten statements, arranged as an outline. For a more complex meeting, the list would be longer.

Start by making a simple list of the points to be made. Assess this list, and rearrange the ideas if necessary so they start at the beginning and move to a logical conclusion. The ideal presentation, long or short, is one the audience finds easy to follow, progresses sensibly, and doesn't skip around. The outline should identify the main points clearly and concisely.

Pinpointing the Visuals

Once satisfied with this embryo script, assess it again—this time to see what needs and opportunities there are for graphic visualizations. Think of four kinds of visuals.

1. Charts, graphs, tables—graphics that carry information. The sales figure for last year, for example; or a graphic comparison of statistics from several years in chart form; or projected sales or profits. Make a note on the script at each point where an informational graphic of some kind is needed.

2. Verbal visuals—the kind in which you list the six cities most eligible for a world's fair 10 years from now, or show the five leading makes of automobiles. Visuals like this consist of lines of type, often with each line numbered. In reality, these are verbal graphs. Make notes in the script margin of where they might be needed.

3. Topical visuals—the ones that carry the topics of the presentation in big, bold type, often with subtopics underneath. A typical visual might

read, "The Automobile Market for 1988." Under this might be subheads referring to the large-car and small-car market share, both of which are subtopics to be covered.

4. Illustrations—visuals for their illustrational value. These should be used only when appropriate. Examples: an aerial view of your company's manufacturing facilities flashed on the screen as you describe them for the audience. Or a photograph of your latest product or a picture of your CEO.

With the possible graphics pencilled in place, the presentation script consists of a list of topic sentences and visuals you believe are needed to carry the presentation. You have what amounts to a rough working draft.

Some General Principles

Some basic principles to keep in mind as this rough working draft develops:

• Visuals are just *carriers* for ideas—and the idea itself is the important thing. A chart, for instance, is a display of an idea. Sales went up, or sales went down; next year promises to be better. Think of the idea the chart is to convey. At this time, forget bars and lines and trick presentation methods. Just focus on the idea. *Every visual should be described on the working script by a sentence that states the idea it is to convey to the audience.*

Don't, for example, note that a "profit chart" is needed. Make the note read, "Chart to show projected improved profits for next year." Then when the chart is made, the operating words will be "improved profits." That's the idea that must get to the audience, and the note will steer the design of the chart later so that it reflects the idea.

• Visuals should emphasize the main points and come on the screen in order. Those that seem unrelated and don't follow one another logically clutter up the presentation, making it hard to follow.

• Don't plan too many visuals. It is impossible to keep any visual on the screen long enough to be appreciated when there are too many in the presentation. Illustrate the high points, not every sentence in the presentation.

• Visuals alone are not the presentation. They only reinforce and clarify it. The real presentation is in the words *plus* the visuals. As with an article in a magazine, the story is in the text; the pictures highlight it. The audience hears what is said—and at the same time sees words or graphics saying the same thing. This is reinforcement that drives the main points of the presentation into their memories. The clarification aspect of visuals is especially important. When presenters talk their way through unillustrated statistics, the audience must struggle to keep the numbers straight. With a good chart on the screen, the presenter can easily conduct a tour of complicated statistics, pointing to each line as it is described, and provide a clear, comprehensive picture.

Finalizing the Script

Every presenter has an individual method of delivery. Some depend on a fully written script which they read or refer to as the presentation progresses. Others work from a topic-sentence outline. Many use the visuals of the presentation as an outline. The verbal side of the script should be prepared to suit the presenter's individual technique. The most convincing delivery usually is done without reading or constant reference to the script. The more presenters appear to be working from their own knowledge of the subject, the better the presentation will be.

The final script can be quite simple or very detailed, as needed. In its leanest form, it should provide a series of topic sentences. It should also show when each visual must be projected on the screen. The script using topic sentences for a typical business meeting probably shouldn't be more than a page or two in length.

A very handy method of preparing the notes when using an overhead projector is to write the outline on the frames of the transparencies. These are easily referred to as the transparency is placed on the stage of the projector.

What Is a Good Visual?

A good visual is meant to assist communication, not take the place of the presenter. The visual clarifies, reinforces, and supplements the text of the presentation for greater impact and memory retention.

A good visual highlights *key* information. It is like the headline on a newspaper story which can only banner the main subject.

A good visual focuses on *one* clear idea. The attention of the audience should be concentrated on one idea, one formula, one key fact. If they get nothing else, the group should absorb that one idea. If three or four ideas appear on the screen at one time, the audience may read one while the presenter talks about another, which destroys the whole idea of reinforcement.

A good visual is simple and accurate—but not necessarily detailed. Show the audience the heart of the idea and fill in the details orally.

A good visual is bold, colorful, informative, and easily read. It is so concise that it can be read with little more than a glance.

When to Use Visuals

The best time to plan the visuals is after developing the total strategy of the presentation. The preparation of a script outlining the ideas facilitates this. After the ideas are lined up, the points at which visuals are needed become apparent. The best reasons to use visuals are:

1. To open the presentation. Use an arresting title or display to get the group's attention.

2. To channel thinking. Select visuals that guide the group's thinking to the conclusions you want them to draw.

3. To emphasize key points.

4. To present financial or statistical data in understandable ways. Masses of numbers can become meaningless when presented orally. Depicted on a graph, they take on meaning.

5. To make comparisons. (This year versus last year, for example.)

6. To show relationships.

7. To simplify complex processes. The "buildup" or "revelation" techniques can be very useful here. Begin with the first step of the process and build the other steps as you explain how it functions.

8. To explain new concepts. Pictures and diagrams can be very helpful when explaining details.

9. When an object is too big or too small to bring to a meeting, show photographs. Examples: a steam roller or a microchip.

Color in Graphics

Color has impact. It has emotional appeal. People respond to it. Given the choice, they will select color over black and white as they did when color was introduced to television. Color brightens a presentation, and people pay more attention to it. In addition, color can be used to emphasize a key idea. When four blue lines of type are projected, followed by one in brilliant red, the red type fairly screams "this is important."

A study by the Bureau of Advertising designed to pinpoint the benefits of color versus black and white in magazine advertising showed, among other things, that readership of the copy in a color ad was 80 percent greater; that sales of advertised products increased by 50 to 85 percent when color was used; and the retention of ad content was increased by from 55 to 78 percent. It is reasonable to believe that similar benefits might be expected in visual presentations in color.

Psychologists have demonstrated that when people are accustomed to color, presentations that are not in color receive decreasing attention. In today's world of color printing and color television, everyone has become color oriented, making it imperative to think of color when preparing effective business presentations.

Good Design Criteria for Visuals

To give visuals the effective properties we have discussed, use these guidelines, which apply chiefly to title and word visuals. In the next chapter, we will talk about how to select the right charts, graphs, and tables.

1. Use one idea per visual.
2. Use a maximum of six to seven words per line.
3. Use a maximum of six to seven lines per visual.
4. When illustrations are used, use no more than one per visual.
5. Use hard-hitting straight English. Use the shortest word that will do the job. Avoid technical jargon and corporatese.
6. Make the letters *big* and *readable*. The presenter shouldn't have to read the visual to the audience. It should be readable from any point in the room. One good rule calls for titles and main headings to be 3 inches high when projected in an average business meeting room.
7. Use no more than three sizes of letters per visual. Uniformity makes the visual easier to read.
8. Use color even in type-only visuals, but use no more than four colors on any graphic.

Critiquing the Visuals

In a final critique of any visual, measure its effectiveness by these criteria:

- Is it simple?
- Is it clear?
- Is it visible?

Simplicity

The visual or graph functions like the underlining in a book. It emphasizes. To do so, it needs to be simple, brief, and readable, delivering only the bottom line. When designing the visual, work at condensing, organizing, communicating. Remove every unnecessary element that doesn't contribute to the main thought. Remember that when the visual is on the screen, explanations and expansions can be added orally. The presenter can enlarge on the subject instead of just reading the projected words.

Clarity

The objective is to deliver the message with absolute clarity in the fewest number of words. Hone each line. Select data with care. Summarize. Simplify. Look for ambiguous words. Reach for the words that provide the clearest instant understanding.

Visibility

Every letter on a visual should be easy for anyone in the meeting room to read. Every image should be clearly identifiable. We've seen a good many rules on how to achieve this. One says that the images on a transparency should be readable with the naked eye at 20 feet. Another says that the smallest image on the screen should be 1 inch high for every 30 feet of viewing distance. We have found that the type of image and the design of the visual change the formula so often that all rules of thumb must be adjusted.

An outline map of the United States, for example, is easily viewed from almost any distance. Individual locations on the map, however, are not always easily seen—particularly if a dozen or more places are indicated. In the final analysis, there is only one sure way to judge visibility. Project a sample visual in the room that will be used or one similar to it. View it from different spots in the room to determine if the lettering sizes and images are satisfactory or must be enlarged.

The goal is to enable every person in the room to read the projected message.

Critiquing the Presentation

The final presentation is a balanced combination of words and graphics, put together to achieve the goal that was set when the script was begun. When delivered, the presentation must project a sense of unity, of being an organized whole with a beginning, middle, and end. There should be a sense of steady progression as the presentation unfolds. Key points should be stressed through the use of visuals. When the presentation has reached a near-final state, it should be reviewed critically, to see that:

1. It feels unified. It should be single-minded. It should set out to reach a goal and proceed straight to that goal without deviating. The usual problem, when unity is lacking, is that material which doesn't pertain to the original purpose has crept in. Edit this out.

2. It feels balanced. Each point should be given the right amount of time and emphasis. Sometimes a complex point can take up more time than it deserves. Parts of the presentation can inadvertently be expanded and become more important than they should. Check to see that no single point has more visuals than needed.

3. The emphasis is where it should be. Ask yourself, "What is this presentation supposed to accomplish? What should the group feel when it is finished?" Usually, the problem is that the logic of the presentation requires emphasis on three or four points, but one was somehow underemphasized or overemphasized as the program was put together. Look for the weak area and add a stronger visual.

4. It has a sense of progression, a logical movement to a conclusion. When a presentation lacks a sense of progression, the problem often turns out to be in the conclusion. A presentation should not be allowed to just fade out or dribble to an end. It should come to a definite conclusion that clearly states what was proven or demonstrated. In the case of a presentation to impart information, it should end with a very concise summary. In a sales presentation, it should sum up the merits it has shown and *ask for the order or action of some type.*

Summary

The first step in preparing a presentation is the writing of a rough presentation script that outlines the ideas to be put forth.

The next step is to note in the margins the possible visuals that might illustrate the script. Indicate what the visual should accomplish. The note should read "Five-year profit growth," not just, "Profits chart."

Good Visuals

A good visual assists communication. It clarifies, reinforces, and supplements the words of the presentation.

A good visual highlights *key* information like the headline on a
newspaper story.
A good visual focuses on *one* clear idea.
A good visual is simple and accurate—but not necessarily detailed.
A good visual is bold, colorful, informative, and easily read at a glance.

Functions of Visuals

Open the presentation.
Channel thinking.
Emphasize key points.
Present statistical data in understandable ways.
Make comparisons.
Show relationships.
Simplify complex processes.
Explain new concepts.
Help the audience understand and remember.

Design Criteria for Visuals

One idea per visual.
A maximum of six to seven words per line.
A maximum of six to seven lines per visual.
When illustrations are used, use no more than one per visual.
Use straight English and the shortest words. Avoid jargon.
Use big letters. The audience should be able to read a visual from any
seat in the room.
Use no more than three sizes of letters per visual for uniformity.
Use color when possible—but no more than four colors per visual.
Color has impact and emotional appeal. People respond to it.

Final Presentation Criteria

Feel unified.
Feel balanced.
Have the emphasis in the right places.
Have a sense of progression.
End with a call to action.

11

Charts, Graphs, and Tables

A table is a visual tool for presenting data. A chart or graph is a tool for explaining or comparing data. A table gives facts and figures; a chart or graph (the words are used interchangeably) clarifies and emphasizes the key relationships between them. While charts, graphs, and tables have been in use for many years, they are more valuable today than ever before because they are the best way to consolidate and interpret the avalanche of data now pouring out of computers.

Bert Auger, in an earlier edition of *How to Run Better Business Meetings*, pinpointed some of the problems associated with the use of charts, graphs, and tables in business presentations. "As useful as they are," he said, "these devices frequently are abused and misused, and often are more a detriment than a help to the clear understanding of the group in a meeting. One of my pet peeves is the presenter who uses charts merely as 'pretty pictures' to dress up a presentation. Worse than that is the presenter whose charts are imprecise and distorted. Such charts don't just waste time; they actually give the observer an incorrect impression of the information."

The objectives of this chapter are to show:

1. How to construct meaningful tables.
2. How to use charts, graphs, and tables effectively—and not as time-wasting illustrations.

3. How to select the proper type of chart or graph to do what is needed in your presentation.

The Prime Rule to Remember

When preparing tables, charts, and graphs for a presentation, remember that no graphic representation is useful in and of itself. It is useful only in relation to the idea it illustrates. It is like a photograph of your grandmother. When your mother hands you an old picture of a young lady, it is meaningless—an old snapshot that relates to nothing. But when she tells you that the lady is your grandmother, and that the picture was taken on the old family farm when grandmother was 13, the meaningless picture suddenly becomes precious. It has a relationship.

When you flash a bar chart on the screen and say, "This chart shows our company profits for the past 10 years," you are handing the audience a picture of your grandmother. The chart has practically no use in the presentation except to waste time or show that you have access to annual reports for the past 10 years. However, if you hold the chart on the screen and point out that the greatest growth has taken place in the years when new products were introduced, you have given the chart a relationship and a meaning.

One way to ensure that charts, graphs, and tables in your presentation are meaningful is to describe each in your preliminary working script by a sentence *that states the idea* it is to convey. The script note for making the chart described above might have been, "Chart showing profit increase in new product years compared to other years." An indication in the script that a chart showing 10 years of profits was needed would not have resulted in the meaningful chart necessary here.

No matter what kind of graphic you plan, always ask, "Why is this being shown? What's the idea the audience will get from it?" If you can't define the idea and relate it to the main line of the presentation, then eliminate the graphic.

Tables

A table is a practical way to summarize a mass of data and to make comparisons (Figures 11.1 to 11.3). However, tables shown during a presentation are projected for only a short time, so it is essential to organize their information into a simple, easy-to-read format. The audience doesn't have a lot of time to assimilate the information and perceive any comparisons. Here are guidelines for the use of tables.

• Keep words to a minimum. The moment the table is projected, the audience switches its attention from your words to the words on the table. They will not listen until they have finished reading. The easier it is for them to grasp the purpose of the table and scan the words, the sooner you regain control.

• Minimize figures. Round out big numbers. It is easier to read $420,000 than $419,826.30. Do not use more figures than necessary to achieve your goal. Don't show sales figures for 10 consecutive years if the same task can be performed by showing only the figures for 10 and 5 years ago along with this year's figures.

• Use tables only when other types of charts can't be used to show the data. Tables tend to be much less dramatic than a pie chart or graph.

• Long columns and narrow, crowded columns are difficult to read at a distance. Use an open table with space around the numbers. Keep the labels on the columns simple—one word per column if possible.

• Use color to highlight the important parts of the table.

• Align columns of numbers by decimal points so that the numbers can be compared easily.

• When the table is projected, orally make the point it illustrates while you point to the appropriate figures on the table. Don't let the audience draw its own conclusions.

Bar Charts

Strong bar charts are good for showing comparisons and depicting changes. Bar charts can be horizontal or vertical. They are particularly effective when the bars are shown in a color that contrasts strongly with the color of the background. There are four basic types of bar charts with which to work.

1. Simple, solid bars or columns.

2. Stacked bars or columns in which comparative information is stacked on top of the basic information. Sales for Product A would be the bottom of the column; sales for Product B would be stacked on top, in a different color, to provide cumulative data and product comparison.

3. Grouped bars or columns, in which each column consists of two or more individual bars, in different colors, grouped together. One group might have three columns showing annual sales, annual profits, and annual costs for 1 year. Three groups shown side by side would provide a clear comparison for a 3-year period.

4. Sliding bar charts have a center line, with bars extending to either side. The center line is the norm, and the length of the bar to either side

_____ DIVISION
$ Millions

	1986	1987 Est. Act.	1988 F'cast	1992 F'cast
U.S. Sales				
Profits				
%				
OUTSIDE U.S. Sales				
Profits				
%				
WORLDWIDE Sales				
Profits				
%				

Figure 11.1

_____ DIVISION – U.S. Consolidated
$ Millions

	1985	1986	1987 Est. Act.	1988 F'cast
Sales				
% Increase				
Profit				
% Increase				
Profit % to Sales				
% Return on Capital Employed				
Capital Turnover				
Cash Contribution Before Dividends				

Figure 11.2

shows how much above or below the norm the data go. If the average temperature in a manufacturing facility should be 72 degrees, the bars could show how many hours above and below this level the temperature deviated from 72.

For the sake of readability, limit all charts to five bars. In all cases, make the bars wide and strong for good visibility.

Pie Charts

Pie charts are a good way to show the relationships of the parts to a whole at a given time. A pie chart, for example, provides a quick visual

_____ DIVISION
Consolidated U.S. Profit & Loss
$ Millions

	1986 Actual	1987 F'cast	1987 Est. Act	1988 F'cast
Net Sales				
Manufacturing				
%				
Laboratory				
%				
Engineering				
%				
Sales Costs				
%				
Administration				
%				
Freight				
%				
Operating Profit				
%				

Figure 11.3

image of market share. The pie represents the entire market; the share of each competitor in the market is shown as a slice of the pie.

For clarity, limit a pie chart to six slices. Give each slice a different and contrasting color. For emphasis, you can explode the pie—pull one slice out slightly. For purposes of comparison, more than one pie chart can be put on the screen at a time, but for the sake of visibility as well as effectiveness, limit the number to two or three pies. Otherwise, the audience will need too much time to study and compare the pies.

Line or Mountain Graphs

Line and mountain graphs are effective for showing changes over many time segments, and also in showing trends. Line graphs consist of one or more lines which flow across the chart. Mountain graphs are the same, except that the area under each line is colored, giving the graph the appearance of a line of mountains.

- Limit any graph to a maximum of six lines. The fewer the better, for the sake of easy readability.
- Make all lines thick enough to be seen easily from a distance.
- Use different colors for each line when more than one appears on the graph.
- In mountain graphs, use contrasting colors for good visibility.

Maps and Other Visual Charts

To spice up a presentation, there are times when art graphics can be used as charts in place of lines or bars. For example, a chart showing the increase in plant employees over a 10-year period might show three figures of workers: a small one representing the number of plant employees 10 years ago; a larger one showing plant employees 5 years ago; and the largest figure showing today's plant employment.

Art graphics used as charts are both good and bad. Good because they can be fresh and different, and give the presentation a lift. Bad because they often are imprecise in depicting information, since it is impossible to create an art graphic that depicts a true comparison. On a bar chart, one bar is visually twice as high as another and the viewer readily sees the comparative value. But when a picture of a worker is twice as tall as another, it appears to be more than double in value because the viewer sees not only the height but also the volume of the drawing. Optically, the larger figure may look three times the size of the smaller. In addition, art visuals usually are more costly and take longer to produce than charts or graphs.

Maps, however, are staples for presentations. They provide instant recognition and quickly pinpoint geographical locations. To be effective, maps must be large enough to be read from the back of the room, and preferably should be in color. When showing specific locations—sales territories, for example—each area should be shown in a separate color to draw attention to it. Lines across maps to illustrate details like travel routes or lines of communication must be heavy and in contrasting colors for high visibility. If there are too many lines, the map loses its significance to the audience.

One way to simplify a map visual is to break it down. For example, to show national sales coverage for a company with six sales divisions, a separate visual might be used for each of the territories. Then a final composite visual could show the map of the entire country with each sales division in a different color. This combination would provide detailed information first, followed by an overview to provide a full perspective.

Diagrams

Diagrams are a concise way to show complex structures and make it possible to understand them at a glance. A corporate organization chart is a good example because in one, the viewers see not only the names and titles of company officers, but also the hierarchical structure. Typical useful diagrams include flowcharts, PERT charts, and decision trees—all of which are hard to explain in words but easy to show in diagram form. Creating a diagram isn't difficult as long as you remember that a diagram has a logic that must be shown. The logic of an organization chart is the chain of command; the logic of a flowchart is the order of events. The graphic must show the logic in an undistorted way. Logically, the president can't be put at the bottom of an organization chart, nor a flowchart started at any point except the first step in the process.

Diagrams should be as simple as possible. If they are too complex, they become difficult to read and absorb the attention of the audience for too long. Faced with a very complicated diagram, break it into parts and show them successively. For instance, show diagrams of individual corporate divisions instead of the entire structure. If there is a need to show the entire company, do that as the last visual in the series, when the audience has already seen the divisions.

Words on Charts and Graphs

Words play an interesting role in any chart or graph. A chart or graph is a picture, and its first impression is that of a picture. Then an explanation of the picture is needed, so the viewer's eye hunts for words to clarify the picture. The sequence in the viewer's mind is like this:

1. A pie chart. It is comparing something. I can see the different divisions.
2. What is the pie chart about?
3. What does each slice represent?
4. What is the overall meaning?

This series of thoughts takes place in microseconds, but the order in which they take place is important. The moment the viewer identifies the type of chart, his or her eye should be able to travel to a title that clearly tells what the chart is about. The best place for the title, most of the time, is at the top of the chart—and the title should be big and easy to read, with the fewest possible number of words. "Market Share" is a good, crisp title. "Share of the Market for Each Manufacturer" is not a good title. Reduce each title to the simplest, clearest words that describe what the chart depicts. If more explanation is necessary, give it orally after the visual is on the screen.

The most common error in lettering charts and graphs is to make the labels—words at the tops of columns, numbers beside a graph, dates at the bottom of a chart, etc.—too small. They should not be as large as the title of the visual, but must be large and bold enough to be read by everyone in the room. They should be restricted to key words or numbers. Abbreviate when possible. For instance, a big FEB is better than a smaller February. Letters and numbers should always read horizontally. Don't permit them to run vertically up the side of the chart so viewers must tilt their heads to read them.

The legend is the part of a chart which tells the viewer what the coloring or shading means, or indicates the chart's scale. Yellow might be sales figures from the Eastern Division; green from the Central.

Some charts work better for certain tasks, which is why there are different kinds of charts. To help select the best type of chart or graph for presentations, here are some very basic guidelines. They are illustrated in Figure 11.4.

1. To show *one* thing, *one* time. To show the parts of a whole, use a pie chart (Example 1) or horizontal bar graph (Example 2).
EXAMPLE: To show the cost of travel as a percentage of sales costs in a

Figure 11.4
FOUR TYPES OF COMPARISON.

1. **To show *one* thing, *one* time:**
   - **Use a pie chart or a horizontal bar chart.**

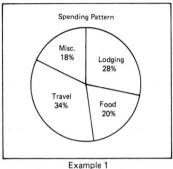

Example 1

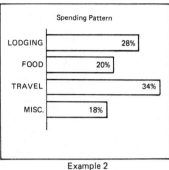

Example 2

Note that the pie chart focuses on each item as a fraction of the whole, while the bar chart focuses on each item relative to the other items. Also note how shading focuses on the large segment, "Lodging," in both charts.

2. **To show *many* things, *one* time:**
   - **Use horizontal bar charts.**

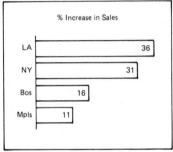

Example 3

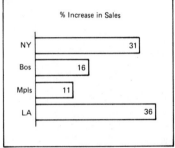

Example 4

Example 3 focuses on relative performance in four markets. Suppose, however, a new sales program had been phased in 4 years ago in the New York Market, 3 years ago in Boston, 2 years ago in Minneapolis, 1 year ago in Los Angeles. Example 4 shows that depicting sales growth chronologically focuses on the success of the new sales program in Los Angeles.

   - **Use double bar charts to focus on two relationships.**

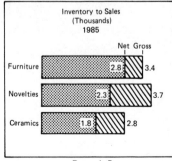

Example 5

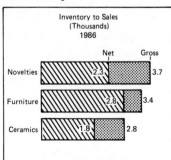

Example 6

Compare Example 5 to Example 6. Example 5 uses darker shading and arrangement of the bars to place primary focus on net investments, which in Example 6 receives only secondary focus.

- **Use sliding bar charts to focus on more than one relationship.**

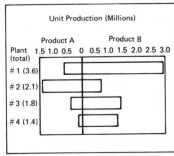

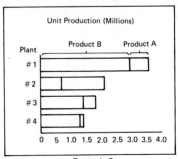

| Example 7 | Example 8 |

Example 7 focuses primarily on these relationships among the four plants: (1) relative production of product A; (2) relative production of product B; (3) relative portion of total production devoted to each product. Secondary focus on total production is provided by the length of the bars and the parenthetical figures. Compare Example 7 to Example 8, in which the double bar chart shifts primary focus to total production.

3. **To show *one* thing *many* times, use vertical bar charts or line charts.**
   (Note the pattern: Comparisons at a point in time use horizontal bars; comparisons over time use vertical bars.)

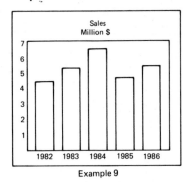

| Example 9 | Example 10 |

Examples 9 and 10 show that if the "many times" are not *too many*, bar charts are preferable to line charts. Example 9 indicates a steady, year-by-year increase in sales from 1982 through 1984. So does Example 10. But the line chart also suggests a steady increase in sales throughout the 2-year period. This may not be true. In Example 9, we see that it is, indeed, not true.

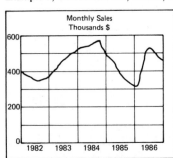

| Example 11 | Example 12 |

To focus on annual comparison, use the bar chart as in Example 9. To focus on monthly trends, use the line chart as in Example 11. Modification of Example 11, shown in Example 12, directs focus to both the annual and the monthly comparisons.

(Continued)

4. To show many things, *many* times, use vertical bar charts or line charts.

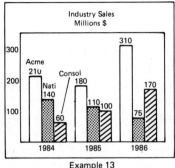

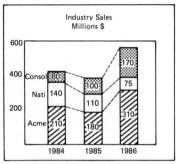

Example 13   Example 14

Example 13 uses shading and grouping of bars to focus on (1) the trend of each firm's sales; (2) the dominance of Acme; and (3) the overtaking of declining National by growing Consolidated. In Example 14, the same data are charted, but the bars are stacked. Note the change in focus to (1) the trend of total industry sales and (2) the relative market share for each firm each year. Note also the change in shading of each firm's bar.

Example 15   Example 16

Very many time periods require the use of line charts as in Example 15. Note the use of broken and dotted lines; this prevents confusion when lines cross. Line charts, like bar charts, may be stacked, as in Example 16, which depicts the same data as in Example 15. Use of heavy verticals facilitates annual comparisons.

regional office, the pie might be broken in the following slices: facilities, salaries and commissions, telephone, office operation, and travel and entertainment. Each slice might be in a different color. The "travel" slice could also be "exploded" or lifted out of the pie slightly.

2. To show *many* things, *one* time. When comparing many items to each other at a specific period of time, use horizontal bar graphs (Examples 3 and 4).

EXAMPLE: Four regional sales offices had an increase in sales last year. Use a horizontal bar graph, letting each bar stand for the percentage increase of one office. This provides a quick visual comparison.

• To focus on *two or more relationships*. Use stacked bar charts (Examples 5 and 6): Show one relationship by the length of the bars, the others by the internal divisions of each bar.

EXAMPLE: To relate inventory to sales in three product categories, use a bar for each product category. The bottom of each bar shows amount of inventory maintained, while the extended part of the bar shows sales. The relationships among the figures are quickly seen and understood.

• To focus on *more than one relationship*. When there are opposing factors, use a sliding bar chart (Example 7).

EXAMPLE: To compare unit production for two products at four plants, use a sliding bar chart (Example 7). The bar to the right of the center line could represent the increase in product B, to the left product A. Use one bar for each plant. The chart will show at a glance (1) the increase in production of the two products and (2) the production of the two products in different plants. Sliding bar charts work well wherever opposing factors must be compared: rainy day sales/dry day sales, in a retail-store sales chart, for example, or credit card sales/cash sales.

The same type of data may also be presented in either a horizontal or vertical stacked bar chart (Example 8).

3. To show *one* thing *many* times. To show the change in value of an item over a period of years, use bar (Example 9) or vertical line (Example 10) bar charts.

EXAMPLE: To compare sales figures over a 5-year period, use (1) a bar chart with a bar for each year. The chart will instantly demonstrate that costs have been rising, falling, or staying the same. (2) The same data can be presented in a vertical line chart.

4. To show *many* things *many* times. When comparing many items over a period of years, use a grouped bar chart (Example 13), a stacked bar (Example 14) chart, or a line chart (Examples 15 and 16).

EXAMPLE: There are five major companies competing in a market. To show how the market share of each has changed over the past 3 years, use:

a. grouped bars—a good graphic representation except when many components must be shown. In this case, five components may be difficult to see. Consider using only the three leading companies to simplify the bars.

b. line chart—using a line of a different color for each company. As long as there is enough separation between the lines, the line chart is effective. When the lines are too close together to be meaningful, increase the scale of the chart. Measure in millions instead of tens of millions, for example.

5. To *compare more than one category* of precise data, use a table.

% Total Sales by Region

	U.S.	Europe	Asia
1982	85	11	4
1983	83	11	6
1984	80	14	6
1985	79	12	9
1986	81	11	8

EXAMPLE: To show U.S., European, and Asian sales and demonstrate the role of each in total sales over a period of years, use a table with columns representing sales dollars or percentages for each year, and lines for each sales category and total sales. This will provide the audience with a quick way of making comparisons and understanding the role of each profit segment in the overall picture. Keep projected tables simple and easy to read.

There are other types and variations of charts, but we recommend these because they are proven in business meeting use, familiar to everyone, and easiest to design and produce. When a group is presented with an unfamiliar chart format, its first reaction is to examine the chart itself rather than its content—a distraction you can do without.

Since there is a wide choice of charts with which to work, there usually is no problem in assembling a variety to keep the presentation alive and interesting. Use color to vary the slides, too—using dark backgrounds for some, light for others.

Distributing Copies of Visuals

We have found it a good idea to give the audience printed copies of visuals used in a presentation to add to their meeting notes. One advantage of overhead projection is that copies of overhead transparencies for distribution can be made quickly on a plain-paper copier. However, it is better not to hand out copies of visuals before or during a presentation for two reasons. The audience will pay better attention during the meeting if they haven't seen the visuals beforehand and—more important—your interpretation of the visuals may be different from the one the group might make before hearing you. They should hear what you have to say first.

Distribute handouts before or during a meeting only if they are needed during the meeting for note taking or feedback. All others should be distributed after the meeting to reinforce the message.

Charts and Graphs Can Distort

If all the numbers are correct, how can a chart or graph distort the true facts? Most seem like straightforward representations of data or information.

In dealing with visuals, we need to remember that the audience's first and major impression is *not* of numbers. It is of the relationships shown by the chart elements. Viewers first sense a comparison and the relative condition of the items being compared. This impression is a lasting one and probably the one which is carried away from the meeting. The figures are secondary to this first impression and often are not what is remembered.

So when designing a chart or graph, think of the *impression* it will create. If illustrating a dip in profits for the summer months last year, the way the chart is constructed can determine how the group sees that dip. It can look like a tremendous drop, a substantial dip, or a moderate dip—according to the way the line on the chart looks. The first step in creating a chart is to select the vertical and horizontal scales—and the scales chosen can change the appearance of the chart significantly, as can be seen in Figure 11.5.

The data used in all three of these charts are the same, but look at the difference in impression! There is no rule we know of to guide the creation of charts and graphs that fairly depict the data. It is a matter of the chart designer's judgment. But every chart should be eyed critically before it is used to look for distortions. Does the chart truly depict the situation it represents? Or does it exaggerate or minimize the facts? Changing a distorted chart usually is just a matter of changing either the horizontal or vertical axis.

Summary

No graphic representation is useful in and of itself, but only in relation to the idea it illustrates.

Figure 11.5
TRAPS TO AVOID

1. The Broken Scale

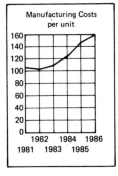

Example 1

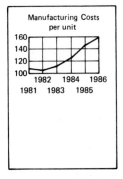

Example 2

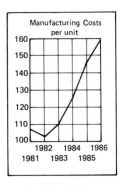

Example 3

Example 1 shows a 49% price increase (from 107 to 159). Since all the action is in the top part of the chart, why not break the scale at 100 and throw away the bottom part? This produces the chart in Example 2. The data are the same, but the eye compares vertical distances and sees an increase of 743% (from 7 to 59). With extra space available, we can lengthen the scale to produce the third chart, Example 3. All three charts show the same data, but only the first chart gives an accurate impression.

2. The Inconsistent Scale

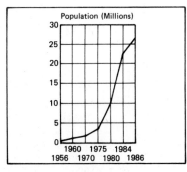

Example 4

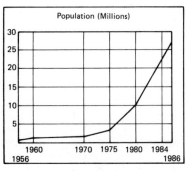

Example 5

In the first chart, Example 4, years for which there were no data are omitted from the time scale. Result: The same distance may represent 2, 3, 5, or 10 years. The second chart, Example 5, uses a consistent time scale. Result: More accurate focus on the key relationship—healthy growth for the first 20 years, spectacular growth in the last 10.

(Continued)

3. Pictorials

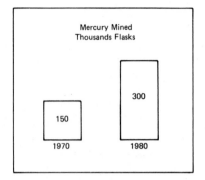

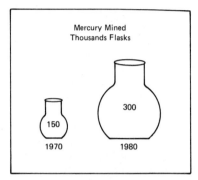

Example 6

Example 7

In the first chart, Example 6, the doubling of quatity mined is simply and accurately emphasized by drawing one bar twice as high as the other. In an attempt to dress up the presentation, the second chart, Example 7, uses flasks, one twice as high as the other. The diameter of the second flask also is twice as great as that of the first, and its volume, which the eye would perceive, is actually eight times as great as the volume of the first. Keep the chart simple. Use bars.

4. Multiple Scales

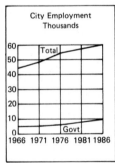

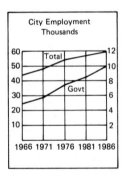

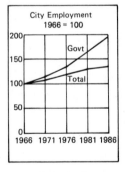

Example 8

Example 9

Example 10

The first chart, Example 8, is unsatisfactory if the key relationship between the two types of employment is their growth, because one is so much smaller than the other. Often, this problem is attacked by using two scales, as in the second chart, Example 9. This approach complicates the chart without focusing on the key relationship, because the viewer is still given a comparison of amounts and in a confusing manner. In the last chart, Example 10, the data are indexed. The chart is simpler, it focuses on relative growth, and the common starting point of its two lines makes comparison clearer.

Types of Visuals

Tables summarize data and make comparisons.

Bar charts show comparisons and depict change. Bar charts can be either horizontal or vertical.

Pie charts show the relationships of parts to a whole at a given time.

Line and mountain graphs show changes over many time segments, and show trends. Line graphs have one or more lines which flow across the chart. In mountain graphs the area under each line is colored.

Art visual charts can be used occasionally in place of line or bar charts.

Maps are staples for presentations, quickly pinpointing geographic locations.

Diagrams are a concise way to show complex structures. Diagrams include organization charts, flowcharts, PERT charts, and decision trees.

Lettering

The most common error in lettering charts and graphs is to make the labels—words at the tops of columns, numbers beside a graph, dates at the bottom of a chart, etc.—too small.

What Type of Chart to Use

1. To show *one* thing, *one* time, such as parts of a whole, use a pie chart or horizontal bar graph.

2. To show *one* thing *many* times, such as the value change in an item over a period of years, use vertical lines or bar charts.

3. To show *many* things *one* time, as when comparing many items to each other at a specific period of time, use horizontal bar graphs.

4. To show *many* things, *many* times, as when comparing many items over a period of years, use a stacked bar chart, a grouped bar chart, or a line chart.

5. To focus on *two or more relationships*, use stacked bar charts. Show one relationship by the height of the bars, another by the internal divisions of each bar.

6. To focus on *more than one relationship* where there are opposing factors, use a sliding bar chart.

7. To *compare more than one category* of precise data, use a table.

12
Making and Ordering Visuals

The explosive rise in the business meeting use of visuals in recent years is related in large part to advances in audiovisual technology which have made slides and transparencies much easier to acquire, less costly, and quicker to produce. There has been a nice synergism at work: as the demand for visuals increased, more research and development was devoted to them; and as more research and development made them more readily accessible, the demand grew.

Executives and managers, engrossed in their own businesses, usually are not aware of the advancing audiovisual technology—so this chapter is devoted to describing the current state of the art of creating and/or ordering 35-mm slides and overhead transparencies.

Anyone ever faced with preparing a presentation knows that the first problem has always been, "How will I produce the visuals?" In the past, this meant, in a large corporation, calling in the art or visual aid department. In a smaller business, it meant contacting an artist or keyliner, photographer, and processor to make arrangements for slide production. An ordinary presentation often was escalated to the status of a large project because of the time and expense of getting ready for it. Many times it was easier to skip the visuals than to go through this ordeal.

Today, producing visuals for a presentation is simple, easy, and inexpensive:

1. Overhead transparencies can be made electronically right in the office on economical, stand-alone plotters with self-contained software that are about the size of a typewriter (Figure 12.1).

2. Overhead transparencies can be made manually in the office, using the plain-paper copier and kits that contain all the material needed to create high-quality originals.

3. Slides and overhead transparencies can be computer-generated and provided by specialized graphic services. They can be ordered by phone, from a service representative or through a microcomputer or terminal over phone lines, and be delivered, ready for projection, in as little as 2 days.

4. Slides can be generated by a microcomputer with graphics capabilities in your office, photographed from the screen, and processed immediately or within hours.

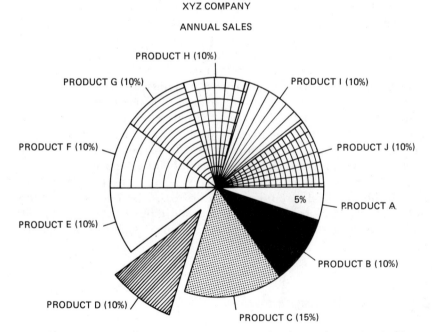

Figure 12.1 Sample of an overhead transparency produced on a plotter using, in this case, 3M plotter film. Most plotters offer at least four-color capability.

5. In-house graphics production equipment that provides complete visual production—from the design to the processed visual—can be installed if the need is great enough.

Do-It-Yourself Transparencies

To begin at the bottom of the visual acquisition ladder, basic kits are available that contain everything necessary to make overhead transparencies manually. The kits include master originals of standard chart and graph formats, rub-on transfer lettering, adhesive film for adding color, mounting frames, colored tapes for lines on charts, etc., as well as templates of uniform symbols. The master originals of often-used chart and graph formats are preprinted, ready for reproduction on the office copier. Appropriate headlines, numbers, and data are then filled in. The graphic original is reproduced on special transparency film on the plain-paper copier—and is ready for projection. A dozen or more overhead transparencies can be made in a couple of hours.

Lettering machines cut the time required to make transparencies manually by producing neatly aligned and spaced letters in a variety of typefaces, sizes, and colors. This eliminates the one-at-a-time transfer of letters to the original. Titles and legends are typed on the machine which makes an adhesive lettered tape which is put in place on the visual. A desktop infrared transparency maker can simplify the process even more. Small enough to fit on the corner of a desk, these machines make transparencies from original art on infrared film in as little as 4 seconds.

However, the manual production of visuals is becoming a thing of the past. Materials will continue to be available for occasional or emergency manual use, but the acquisition of visuals—either 35-mm slides or overhead transparencies—has moved rapidly into electronics and computer generation, which offer so many advantages that they have become the standard way for most businesses. The visuals from these systems are professional in appearance and can be delivered in less time than it takes in most cases to produce a similar quality visual by older methods.

Electronic Transparencies

Electronic transparency makers are instruments that reduce the time required to produce overhead transparencies of tables, graphs, and charts to just minutes. Similar to plotters which reproduce graphics from a computer screen, these small units have built-in computers. The software contains a wide selection of standard chart and graph formats. The operator need only answer a few questions in response to questions from the computer, then type in the chart data. The transparency maker automatically selects type styles, colors, layout, and positioning for each chart—or the operator can direct it in this selection.

Automated ink pens containing colored inks, guided by the computer's software, draw the visual on transparency film on the plotter bed. Any chart can be stored in memory or on tape and be recalled for editing or last-minute changes. The automatic drawing of the chart takes only a few minutes, and the transparency is ready for projection when it comes from the plotter table.

Electronic transparency makers are desktop size, portable, and can be operated by anyone after a short training period. Transparencies for a typical presentation can be made in an hour or a little more—but the operator is free to do other things while the plotter pens are at work.

Electronic transparency makers (Figure 12.2) can also produce colored paper copies of transparencies for distribution to those attending

Figure 12.2 Producing overhead transparencies on a plotter is one way to produce crisp, colorful, and professional-looking business graphics.

meetings. They also can be connected by phone to a computer-generated slide service, so 35-mm visuals of the same data can be ordered.

Computer-Generated 35-mm Slides

Computer-generated 35-mm slides of charts, tables, and graphs have now become a standard for business meeting graphics and can be produced on a microcomputer or ordered through a computer-generated graphics service. If your microcomputer has graphics capabilities and the proper software, the slides can be created on the screen, then photographed by special equipment on 35-mm film. After normal photo processing, the slides are ready. Software now available does much of the design work and simplifies the system. Normal acquisition time, including processing, is 1 to 2 days.

For meetings in offices where a microcomputer is located, there has been an increase in the use of graphics used right on the computer screen to illustrate presentations, eliminating the need for slides or transparencies. Because of the screen size, the technique is effective for meetings involving no more than six or seven persons. It requires preprogramming of the computer to design the graphics and establish the order in which they appear, which can be time-consuming. However, this method is another step toward bringing visuals to every meeting to increase efficiency and productivity.

Computer Graphics Services

Recognition of the tremendous growth in the use of visuals at business meetings has prompted the growth of professional computer graphics services whose main business is to design and produce slides and transparencies to order. The quality of these slides is high and the service fast—varying, of course, from one service to the next. Visuals usually can be delivered, ready to project, in 1 to 10 days, depending on urgency and the customer's willingness to pay rush charges.

Depending on the service, slides are ordered by telephone through a microcomputer terminal or word processor with a modem—or by a regular phone call—or from a representative of the service who picks up the order at your office. The ordering process is easy. The types of charts or graphs are selected from a sample group, and the customer provides the chart data. This information is entered into a computer at the service's plant, and the slides are automatically made and processed.

3M's own Meeting Graphics Service (Figure 12.3) is nationwide and delivers finished slides or overhead transparencies in 2 days or less by express service. On joining the service, members receive a format guide—a sample book showing more than 100 different formats, including titles, text, tab charts, vertical and horizontal bar charts, line graphs, pie charts, and special effect graphics. The visuals are ordered through a personal computer, word processor, or any communications terminal.

Graphic formats are selected from numbered examples in the format guide, and slide data are provided by answering questions on the easy-to-complete worksheets. The MGS computer automatically proportions the material on each visual for maximum readability, and the slides or transparencies are automatically produced and shipped. Visuals are

Figure 12.3 Ordering 35-mm slides by computer and telephone modem from 3M's Meeting Graphics Service. Slides, overhead transparencies, or paper copies are shipped to the customer within 48 hours or sooner if desired.

stored in the computer's memory and can be called back for late changes or replicated for use in later presentations. The cost of the service is less than that of professionally produced slides using older methods. After an initial sign-on fee, users pay only for each visual ordered. The service also provides color prints and hard copies of visuals in any quantity for meeting distribution.

Automated Transparency- Making Equipment

If the need for overhead transparencies and colored paper prints is large enough, automated equipment that will reproduce them right in the office can be installed. Units about the size of a console-type plain-paper copier (Figure 12.4) make up to 50 color prints or 40 transparencies an hour. The equipment is microprocessor-controlled, self-contained, and no more difficult than a plain-paper copier to operate. The prints and transparencies come out of the machine dry and ready to use. The equipment makes full-color transparencies from 35-mm slides and any printed material up to 8½ by 11 inches in size.

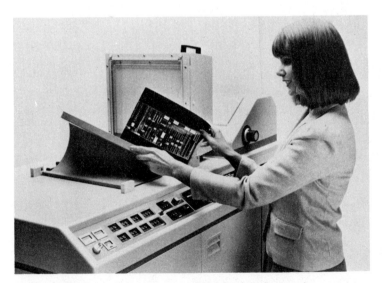

Figure 12.4 Several manufacturers offer full-color photographic transparency makers. Full-color transparencies add enormous visual impact to presentations. Because the equipment is expensive, graphics of this type may be obtained at various service centers around the country.

Full-Color In-House Visual Services

For companies with very large 35-mm slide, overhead transparency, and color print needs, equipment that offers complete in-house production capability is available. These units have computer design facilities and a designer's workstation as well as completely automated processing capabilities. They can produce 35-mm slides, overhead transparencies, and color prints. A skilled operator is required, but for organizations which use large numbers of graphics daily or have security concerns, in-house workstations offer advantages.

In some cases, graphics can be ordered from these workstations by a terminal that communicates with a distant processor. This avoids the necessity of installing the equipment locally, and delivery of the visuals is by mail or express service.

The Outlook for the Future

The technology of graphics production has advanced rapidly in recent years, and the advances continue as the use of visuals escalates. The aim of researchers and developers has been to produce better looking visuals of all types, get them to the user faster, and to keep the cost of production down. Anyone using visuals should watch for new developments in this field. The services and equipment we have discussed here are only an indication of the direction in which visuals are headed.

Summary

Professional-looking 35-mm slides and overhead transparencies can be produced easily, quickly, and inexpensively today by:

Manual production of overhead transparencies. Complete kits with the basic materials needed for do-it-yourself production of visuals are available. These can be augmented by lettering machines and desktop transparency makers to speed production.

Electronic production of overhead transparencies. Desktop electronic transparency makers automatically draw charts, graphs, and titles in color on transparency film in minutes.

Computer-generated 35-mm slides. Slides and overhead transparencies can be computer generated by specialized graphic services, ordered by phone from a service representative, or through a microcomputer or terminal over phone lines and delivered in as little as 2 days.

In-house production facilities for overhead transparencies. Self-contained in-house units that make transparencies and color prints and operate as easily as plain-paper copiers are available.

In-house design and production of 35-mm slides, overhead transparencies, and color prints. For those with high-volume needs, workstations that are complete visual "factories" are available.

13

Specialist and Technical Presentations

If you are a professional—an engineer, scientist, economist, controller, statistician, biologist, mathematician, computer programmer, or other technical person—you are a part of a growing band of people who are reshaping the world. You are part of a powerful force in the conduct of business. You are one of the new communicators. You have a message people are waiting to hear. You are a part of the scientific and technological wave which has created entirely new industries and reshaped or outdated old ones. You are in the vanguard of dramatic new things to come.

Your Achilles heel, if you have one, is that you haven't learned to communicate very well beyond the confines of your specialty. This may serve if you are content to stay in the laboratory or at the computer console. But to step across the threshold of management, you must assume responsibilities for communication to those beyond your professional specialty—and for selling as well as communicating. You need to be able to handle the nontechnical and the technical presentation with equal dexterity.

"In" Languages

A dialect, according to *Webster's New Collegiate Dictionary*, is a regional variety of language distinguished from other regional varieties by

167

features of vocabulary, grammar, and pronunciation. The dictionary adds that a variety of language used by members of an occupational group is also a dialect. This is the formal way of describing what most of us call an "in" language. There are as many dialects of the English language as there are scientific and other disciplines. Every profession has its own, and it is difficult if not impossible for persons outside the discipline to understand it. To specialists or technical people, this language is natural and easy but becomes a severe communications block when they make presentations to people outside the discipline.

An "in" language contains many words and phrases with special meanings that have been developed as language shortcuts. The use of an "in" language and its specialized terminology can be attributed to various factors—just plain habit, the desire to impress others, or perhaps a witting or unwitting attempt to be obscure. Whatever the reason, the use of this kind of language in nontechnical presentations results in poor and ineffective communication, and is a high price to pay. It seldom impresses anyone, and almost always is confusing. On the other hand, everyone enjoys the bright light of understanding that switches on when an unknown is explained and becomes clear.

Lay Audiences versus Scientific Audiences

People sometimes distinguish between "lay" audiences and, for example, "scientific" audiences, basing the distinction on the "language" the audience understands. There is an assumption that all scientific audiences understand any presentation made in a language full of complex scientific terms. This is an oversimplification because the language problem goes deeper than that. A chemist using the dialect of his or her discipline can communicate with other chemists, but probably won't be able to communicate with biologists, computer specialists, or engineers. So the first rule of presentations for a specialist is:

> Always speak in the language of the audience. Adjust the language of any presentation made to persons not of your own specialty so the audience can understand it.

The Bilingual Specialist

A specialist using an "in" language to a business group must stop and explain specialized terms. But at a scientific meeting, this specialist would appear foolish or to be talking down to the group by making such explanations. Thus the specialist who makes both business and technical presentations must be bilingual—able to speak in both standard English and the dialect of the specialty. Therefore, the second rule of presentations for a specialist is:

> Always use "in" language with insiders of a specialty. This gains better credibility and better communication. However, use simple, nontechnical English when talking to persons outside of the specialty and explain any "in" terminology that must be used.

Selling in the Specialist Presentation

Scientific and technical people frequently make presentations, notably papers outlining their research work, to meetings of their peers, so we tend to assume that they are practiced presenters. However, there is a major difference—aside from language—between a presentation to a group of scientists and one to a group of business people. This difference is in the intent of the presentation.

In almost every business presentation there is an element of persuasion or *sell*. The presenter sells an idea, a plan of action, a change of plans, etc. A business meeting is full of persuasion, both direct and indirect. Decisions are arrived at through persuasion; even "accountability" presentations sell, persuading the group that objectives either were or were not met.

When a chemist, an engineer, a biologist, a computer programmer, or anyone from a scientific discipline presents a paper at a scientific symposium or meeting, however, certain unwritten ground rules must be observed. For one thing, the paper must never *sell*. The presenter must bend over backward to eliminate any unnecessary or unusual emphasis. A biologist, when presenting a report on research work, must explain the step-by-step procedure in great detail. The supposition is that others in the field should be able to duplicate the work. Any conclusions are very carefully drawn and seldom presented in positive, selling terms. A paper, in essence, says, "Here is the work we have done, and here is what we believe it means—subject to further findings."

When this same biologist makes a presentation to other managers within the company, perhaps even on the same research subject, these "peer review" rules can't apply. Within the company, the presentation is likely to be made for economic reasons: why the budget for this research should be extended another year, or why the product developed from the research should do well. In making a presentation to other managers, the technical specialist is almost always selling something: an idea; the belief that the research, though progressing slowly, is on the right track; the need for a new avenue of investigation. Since technical people constantly face "selling" and "nonselling" presentation situations—often on the same subject before different groups—they need to be very aware of the two kinds of presentations and the distinctions between them:

> *The technical presentation*—low key, very factual, a dispassionate presentation of data and methods, delivered in the dialect of the discipline.
>
> *The business presentation*—most often goal-oriented, also factual, but with emphasis designed to sell, persuade, or achieve the goal.

The sum of this is that specialists must know how to make two kinds of presentations involving two languages and two techniques—one to their peers in their own fields and another to persons outside of the discipline.

Accountants and Lawyers Are Technical Specialists, Too

Accountants and lawyers, for some reason, often don't consider themselves very different from other business people and frequently run into the "in" language problem. This becomes evident when members of either profession make presentations to top management. They tend to use accounting or legal terms freely, as if they were a normal part of everyone's language. The result usually is much discussion following the presentation, often because the group didn't understand some of what was said.

Know Your Audience

A presenter must know the audience and tailor the presentation for it. Knowing the audience includes not only being ready to talk to them in their language, but also knowing why they are attending the presentation. The meeting usually revolves around the audiences' "special interest"—be it profits, in the case of management; new-product advantages, for sales and advertising people; or exotic materials, for manufacturing managers. The presentation should address itself specifically to that special interest. The audience needs to share the specialist's special knowledge in relation to their special interest—and no more.

Specialists—and especially technical people—tend to present more information than necessary. An accountant discussing new program costs may carefully spell out last year's model cost as $9,986,875.98, and then break the component costs down further. Yet the audience of marketing managers or manufacturing specialists really needs only a ballpark figure—in this case, $10 million. Lawyers, in speaking of a legal problem, like to cite precedent cases in depth. In their minds, the more such cases there are, the stronger the company's case. But those attending the meeting need only to know that the case is strong, based on precedent. They can be spared the endless details.

Engineers and other technical people like to outline the history of a project because how and why a system or development came about is important to them. The audience, however, needs only a brief review since it doesn't share the presenter's interest in the background of the project. They *do* need to know about the project itself as it affects their work.

Generating a Technical Presentation

To put together a technical presentation for persons outside of your discipline, begin the outline of a presentation by preparing a working script. Ask yourself these questions:

1. What do I want these people to believe when they leave this meeting?
2. What action on their part do I want to generate?
3. What information do I have that will help them to believe what I say and take the action I want?

If you answer these three questions and frame your presentation around them, the "sell" will be built into your script. The key word is *believe.* You may want the financial people to believe your research project is sound and should be continued, or the sales people to believe the product now emerging from research is a world beater. Because of this belief, you want them to commit additional funds. Whatever the goal, fix the idea in your mind at the beginning. Your presentation will then tend to shape itself around your goal orientation.

Chairing the Nontechnical
Technical Meeting

If you are the meeting leader, the best way to begin a meeting—and to eliminate the premeeting jitters every presenter feels—is to project a visual of the agenda on the screen. This quickly focuses the attention of the audience on the business at hand and away from you for a moment. It also tells the audience that you are organized, have lots of things to discuss, and need their attention.

Next, remember that your audience consists of nontechnical people. Prepare a short opening statement which includes a very brief technical background—enough to bring them up to speed and give them a general understanding of the subject. Laypersons in technical meetings often are bashful about asking technical questions when they don't know the technology. They don't want to appear stupid. When someone gets up enough nerve to ask a dumb question, you can see the smiles of relief on everyone else's face. They all wanted an answer to the question but were afraid to ask.

In the opening statement, remember the audience's special interest and relate the technical field to it. Briefly tune them in at the point where your interests and their interests coincide. Then let the meeting roll on.

Making the Nontechnical
Technical Presentation

If you are making a presentation, but not leading the meeting, you come on stage in one of two atmospheres. Either the meeting leader has prepared the group and they understand the context in which your presentation is to be made, or they have been totally bemused by an avalanche of technical concepts and jargon. Good technical presenters have told us they come prepared for either eventuality. If the meeting has gone well to this point, they pick up the beat and launch into their presentations. If the air is full of fog when they reach the podium, they deliver a quick preparatory statement, like the one the meeting leader should have made, before going ahead. Good presenters say they keep these statements in an inside pocket, ready if needed but otherwise ignored.

You will brighten the outlook of a nontechnical audience if the first visual in your presentation is nontechnical. This will give them a chance to warm up to the more complex material to follow. When you get to this technical material, remember that age old saying about a picture being worth a thousand words. *In most presentations, the visuals are intended to supplement what the presenter has to say. In the technical presentation, the reverse is often true.* The picture may be the key while the presenter's words are supplemental.

For example, if an engineer needs to explain a technical point about screws—and why a new type may work better in a product—simple drawings can be projected to introduce the technology of screws (Figure 13.1). The speech might read: "A screw has a cylindrical shank from which a continuous helical rib or thread projects. When designing a screw, it is necessary to consider the pitch, the major diameter, and the minor diameter—all of which affect the characteristics of the screw. Pitch is determined by counting the number of complete revolutions the thread makes per inch. The reciprocal of the number of threads per inch is called the pitch. In addition to the pitch, we must consider the size of the thread on the cylindrical shank. This is done by referring to the bottom portion of each thread as the minor diameter and the peak of each thread as the major diameter."

As the speaker goes on, the audience will find the jargon impenetra-

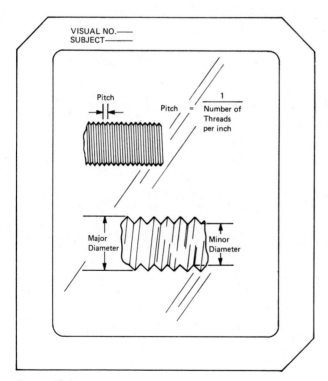

Figure 13.1

ble. Their eyes will be on the pointer, which touches a drawing of a screw on the screen and points to each part of the screw as it is described. The group will hear the words, but most of what they absorb will come from the visual. Without it, they would find this speech impossible to follow. The simple visual illustrates the main points—pitch, major diameter, and minor diameter—and makes the technology simple. By the time this visual is taken down, this nontechnical audience will understand enough about the design of a screw to be ready for the next visual, in which the presenter explains the advantages of changing the screw design in the company's product.

Main Properties of a Nontechnical Technical Visual

The simple visual used in this presentation illustrates several basic points about good nontechnical technical visuals.

1. It shows that the presenter recognizes the audiences' lack of technical knowledge. This visual wouldn't be used before a group of engineers. It's too basic.

2. It is simple enough to be understood even by nontechnical people at a glance.

3. It uses technical terms but it *explains* them at the same time.

4. It has only a few labels, so they can be read quickly.

5. It refers only to the characteristics about which the audience needs to know. The presenter doesn't go into the different types of screw heads, the different metals that might be used, or any other technical material. He talks only of the pitch and diameters because he intends to explain how changing these will affect the product.

6. The idea presented by the visual can be covered quickly, and another visual can then be put up. The longer a technical visual must stay on the screen, the more difficult it is to hold the attention of the group.

Technical Charts and Tables

The rules for making good charts, graphs, and tables covered in Chapter 11 apply equally to visuals in a technical presentation. Since technical material can be rather heavy and static, especially for the nontechnical listener, it is wise if possible to include some visuals to lighten up the presentation. Stick-figure cartoons, used in the right places, or photographs, can help to break up a long chain of charts. Other types of visuals found in technical presentations include the following.

Schematics

Schematic drawings are a concise way to show a complex subject that is almost impossible to describe in words alone. Use them freely in front of technicians, but very sparingly—if at all—in front of nontechnical persons. Only technical people understand the symbolism on a schematic. To show one to a nontechnical audience would require an explanation for each symbol—turning your presentation into Electronics 101 for first-year students. But even when offering a schematic to persons who understand it, be careful not to overload the screen. If discussing the circuitry in a television set, don't try to put the entire electronic map in one visual. Break it down and show it in components.

Block Diagrams

Various kinds of block diagrams can be used to illustrate the order of steps in a process, the flow of work on a line, etc. Because they are flexible, block diagrams offer an excellent means of clarifying many different systems or processes. They can be made to work well for both the technical and nontechnical audience. But as with schematics, if the block diagram covers too much, it loses its efficacy. When you must show a complex system, use several successive block diagrams. If there is a need to show the entire system on one screen, hold that visual until after the group has seen visuals explaining the individual parts. The audience then won't have to read each label, but can look on the visual as an overview.

Working Models

If it is possible to present a working model of the subject of your presentation, consider doing it. However, working models can be seen only by a few of the audience during the presentation and must be shown to the others afterward. Perhaps a better way, if a working model is available, is to shoot a videotape of it in operation, and screen the tape for the group. Such a tape needn't be a big production—just a few minutes in length—and it can be shot without expensive professional assistance.

Technical Presentations
before Technical Audiences

Nothing can be more painful to an audiovisual specialist than to attend a national or international congress in almost any scientific discipline and observe the presentation of papers. The very nature of presentations of this type understandably preclude dramatics, and those attending the congress don't expect them. But they should and do expect to see and understand the visuals of the presentations. Unfortunately, as far as visuals are concerned, these presentations all too often are borderline, at best, and as a general rule, far less than satisfactory.

Scientists we have talked to seem to have an innate feeling that a really good visual presentation is a kind of grandstanding, and that a homemade, laboratory look to the visuals lends authenticity. But when we talk to those in the audience, we find nothing but complaints. One medical researcher at a congress in Japan, when asked about a presentation he had just witnessed, said, "Maybe his work was good. I don't know. I liked the idea but I couldn't see his data. Maybe I can get a copy of his paper."

Our recommendation to those delivering papers is: Follow the guidelines in Chapter 11 and produce the best visuals you can. Those attending the meeting will appreciate understanding your work—even if they don't agree with it.

Equipment for Technical
Presentations

Clearly the overhead projector is the method of choice for most technical presentations. Transparencies can be made quickly and the overhead allows good presentation techniques. Quite often, it makes sense to distribute copies of the visuals after a technical meeting—and these can be quickly and easily made from transparencies. In meetings where there is technical discussion, the ability to write on the transparency while it is being projected can be very useful. Suggested changes in a schematic, for example, can be sketched in on the spot.

Next most useful is the 35-mm slide presentation. While not as flexible as the overhead, the slide presentation is extremely powerful and impressive. Perhaps the best presentation of all is made with a combination of the two techniques, using two screens. The main program can be on the overhead screen, while slides can be introduced on the other screen when they offer the most effective method of making a point.

Summary

Use "in" language only with insiders. Always use simple, nontechnical English when talking to persons outside of your own specialty.

Specialists must know how to make two kinds of presentations—one to their peers in their own fields, and the other to business people outside their field.

The technical presentation is a low key, factual presentation of data and methods, delivered in the dialect of the discipline.

The business presentation is goal-oriented, factual, with emphasis designed to sell, persuade, or achieve the goal.

Know the Audience

A presenter must know the audience and tailor the presentation for it. This includes knowing why they are attending the presentation and using their own language.

Meetings revolve around the audiences' "special interest," and the presentation must address itself specifically to that interest.

How to Begin Making a Technical Presentation

To put together a technical presentation for persons outside of a discipline, prepare a working script. Ask three questions and frame the presentation around the answers:

1. What do I want these people to believe when they leave this meeting?

2. What action on their part do I want to generate?

3. What information do I have that will help them to believe what I say and take the action I want?

Properties of a Nontechnical Technical Visual

- It should indicate that the presenter recognizes the lack of technical knowledge of the group.
- It should be simple enough to be understood quickly by nontechnical people.
- It should avoid technical terms, but may use them if the terms are explained.

- It should have a minimum of labels so it can be read quickly.
- It should refer only to information the audience needs to know—and not an entire technology.
- It should focus on a single idea that can be covered quickly. The longer a technical visual must stay on the screen, the more difficult it is to hold the attention of the group.

14

The Financial Presentation

The chair of the board of a large U.S. corporation once compared the respective roles of the controller and the manager in business to specialists in the medical world. "The controller is the diagnostician," he said, "who determines when and where the company is ill. The manager is the surgeon who operates on that ailment." This is one of the shortest, clearest job descriptions we have heard.

The financial presentation is the vehicle by which the diagnostician reports to the surgeons, and the diagnostician must be able to communicate findings accurately, quickly, and simply so the surgeons can get on with the cure.

In today's fast-paced business world, the need for management awareness is greater than ever before and the role of the financial officer has changed and enlarged. Financial reporting now has a much more active role in the management conference room.

"Today, management lives by the numbers," says Dr. Marshall Hatfield, vice president of 3M's Audio Visual Division. Then he adds, "But financial data and an lysis often can be complex and extremely difficult to understand, and may be a roadblock to effective communication. The financial manager or executive must be able to breathe life into the numbers—let them tell a story that will have meaning and capture the attention of everyone in the meeting. In short, he must be a financial professional, and a communications professional as well."

Financial information must be communicated at every level of management. The information varies in detail and emphasis at each level, but one thing remains the same at all levels—the need to understand the information that is presented. The real danger is that the financial presenter may so overwhelm the audience with masses of figures and analyses of intricate relationships that the information the group really needs is lost. After such a meeting, the financial presenter may be pleased with having made a thorough presentation; members of the group, however, may leave the room in a haze of numbers, with no clear idea of what they came to the meeting to learn.

The financial presenter, regardless of title or level of responsibility, is a specialist and needs to abide by the rules given for specialist presentations in the previous chapter. Most important, he or she must *know* the audience's level of understanding—and what information is important to it. The presentation must be given in terms the group can understand without the services of a translator. And it must offer the specific information needed. If the group is given a mass of data from which the needed information must be extrapolated, the financial presenter has failed in the job.

The Financial Audiences

Within any company, there are a range of audiences. At the top management level, financial presentations must enable management to review and formulate policy and long-range plans. Executives at this level need to know the total earnings position of the company and the contribution made by each of its divisions and product lines to that earning position. Any presentation which clutters up this insight does top management a disservice.

Middle managers have a different problem. They deal with day-to-day specifics—units produced, unit costs, workhours, down time, overtime, etc. Their first job is to be aware of these figures and to maintain and/or improve them. Beyond this, they are in a pivotal position. They receive daily information from their subordinates and must prepare reports for their superiors that translate this information into profit-and-loss terms. They must be financially bilingual, interpreting one level to the other, both coming and going. Presentations to them should recognize the smaller scope of their needs and their special need to translate data as they pass it up or down the chain of command.

Each manager, depending on the individual's level in the organization, needs a different kind of financial information, presented in a different way. The job of the financial presenter is to know exactly what those needs are, and present the relevant data and interpretations in a way that is well understood.

Other financial audiences include the board of directors, the stockholders, and financial analysts outside of the company. Each of these also has a different reason for meeting with financial representatives of the company. The best presentation is the one which is prepared to meet the needs of the audience, whoever they are.

There is no end to the amount of financial information that can be presented to any audience. There is, however, a limit to how much any audience, including your own management, can absorb and act on at any given time. Financial presentations have a reputation for being boring. The reason is twofold: first, too much data, which not only cannot be absorbed but turns off the attention of the hearers; second, data by itself is boring unless it comes alive as a meaningful story.

Guidelines for a Good Financial Report

The key to a good financial report is knowing exactly why the report is to be made. The management group which will hear the report has a specific need for certain information and the successful financial report provides exactly what is needed—and not a whole lot more.

In other words, the surgeons need a diagnosis, and not a course in anatomy.

In an effort to be comprehensive, financial managers sometimes assemble large quantities of data for presentations, feeling the need to show management "the big picture." Unfortunately, to individual managers who are interested only in a square inch or two of the picture, these reports are a headache. The group must sit through a presentation that wastes time, and then cull from it the specific information needed.

One sure measurement of the value of a financial report is the number of questions after the presentation or the phone calls received later. If the group members find it necessary to ask for much clarification, the presentation, no matter how beautiful it was, failed in its primary intent—to provide understandable encapsulated data that permit them to get on with their work.

The following are guidelines for readying a good financial report at any level of management:

- Determine precisely what this group wants to know. What specific figures are essential; what analyses and interpretations are useful.
- Prepare a presentation that offers only what is needed. Eliminate extraneous information.
- Prepare visuals which emphasize the highlights. Don't project whole sheets of computer printout. Avoid projecting crowded typewritten balance sheets. Edit each down to only the essentials, shown in as few lines and columns as possible. While we recommend that no visual have more than six or seven lines, this layout is usually not practical for balance sheets and other financial reports. But with a little thought, simplification usually is possible.
- Round off figures to simplify the presentation. Drop the pennies. Make $502,345 read $500,000 unless there is an important reason to show every dollar. Use $54 million instead of $54,000,000.
- Use normal business language during the presentation. Keep accounting terminology at a minimum.
- In your role as a financial consultant to managers, point out trends or aberrations from the norm. You may be able to provide managers with an early warning of trouble to come and give them the opportunity to take corrective action.

Be Selective with Data

The simpler and more focused the presentation, the better. The financial presenter has hundreds of pieces of information available, but only a handful bear on any particular situation. The most creative job the financial presenter can do is select the meaningful data and present them in sharp focus. This makes for shorter, more lively presentations, and does a better job of preparing the managers for their work as surgeons.

Analyzing Data to Tell a Story

Financial presenters should train themselves to think not of the amount of data that might be displayed, but rather how much useful information can be extracted for management from each bit of data. Accountability or performance charts, for example, make comparisons, but comparisons alone are not the story. They might show that, compared to last month, sales are up and profits remained the same. The statistics themselves are not nearly as significant as the answer to why this occurred.

(a)

ABC COMPANY
1970 P & L STATEMENT

M. DOLLARS

	MAY	JUNE	% CHANGE
SALES	12650	14590	15.3
NET MFG. COSTS	6072	7295	20.1
% TO SALES	48.0	50.0	
LAB & ENGINEERING	1275	1474	15.7
% TO SALES	10.1	10.1	
SALES COSTS	3465	3983	14.9
% TO SALES	27.4	27.3	
ADMINISTRATION COSTS	770	890	15.6
% TO SALES	6.1	6.1	
FREIGHT COSTS	180	220	22.2
% TO SALES	1.4	1.5	
TOTAL COSTS	11762	13863	17.9
% TO SALES	93.0	95.0	
NET PROFIT	888	727	(18.1)
% TO SALES	7.0	5.0	

(b)

ABC COMPANY
BREAKDOWN OF MANUFACTURING COST

M. DOLLARS

	MAY	JUNE
MATERIALS	3160	3650
% TO SALES	25.0	25.0
WASTE	420	770
% TO SALES	3.3	5.3
FACTORY LABOR	545	650
% TO SALES	4.3	4.4
FACTORY OVERHEAD	1530	1745
% TO SALES	12.1	12.0
MAINTENANCE	265	300
% TO SALES	2.1	2.1
SUPPLIES	152	180
% TO SALES	1.2	1.2
NET MEG. COSTS	6072	7295
% TO SALES	48.0	50.0

(c)

ABC COMPANY
WASTE STATEMENT BY PRODUCT & OPERATION

M. DOLLARS

	MAY	JUNE	% CHANGE
PRODUCT A			
DEPT. 01 - PRODUCTION	80	105	31.3
DEPT. 02 - CONVERTING	45	60	33.3
DEPT. 03 - PACKING	15	15	—
PRODUCT B			
DEPT. 01 - PRODUCTION	90	110	22.2
DEPT. 02 - CONVERTING	80	350	337.5
DEPT. 03 - PACKING	15	20	33.3
PRODUCT C			
DEPT. 01 - PRODUCTION	60	70	16.7
DEPT. 02 - CONVERTING	25	30	20.0
DEPT. 03 - PACKING	10	10	—
TOTAL WASTE	420	770	83.3

(d)

ABC COMPANY
DEPT. 02 - CONVERTING

WASTE STATEMENT - PRODUCT B

M. DOLLARS

	MAY	JUNE	% CHANGE
SHIFT 1	25	40	60.0
2	30	270	800.0
3	25	40	60.0

PROBLEM AREA: WASTE IS OUT OF LINE FOR:

PRODUCT B

DEPT. - 02

SHIFT - 1

FOREMAN - SMITH

Figure 14.1

After analyzing the financial data, a controller might plan a series of visuals for a presentation to management that would tell a story:

1. Using a summary profit-and-loss chart, the presenter shows that the improvement in sales was offset by a significant increase in manufacturing costs (Figure 14.1a).

2. Figure 14.1b shows a breakdown in manufacturing costs. It clearly shows that waste costs for the period were out of line.

3. Figure 14.1c depicts a breakdown of waste costs. It is immediately

apparent that the waste converting operation for product B jumped tremendously during this month.

4. The final visual in the series, Figure 14.1d, zeroes in on the waste conversion operation of product B. The problem has now been pinpointed to the second shift, where something has gone wrong.

Here, in four well-planned visuals, the controller has analyzed a low-profit situation for management and reported it in simple, easy-to-appreciate form. The presentation has a clear story line that begins with the problem and quickly narrows down to its source. There is no unnecessary information, no wasted time. Now the manufacturing people know where to look to solve the problem. Rather than hand them the big, broad statement that the "manufacturing costs went up"—the point where many financial presentations stop—the controller here has gone on to show them where to perform their surgery. The maximum amount of information has been extracted from the statistical information.

Visual Techniques

The most important idea to grasp is that a financial presentation is not a display of mere numbers but one of ideas. The visuals in a financial presentation must, of course, be built with numbers, but they should demonstrate ideas. It is one thing to project a chart showing that overtime hours have increased. It is quite another to lay two more lines on the chart—one showing what will happen in the future if these costs continue to rise and another showing what might happen if these hours were trimmed. The first chart contains meaningful numbers. The second chart contains the same numbers but translates them into meaningful ideas.

In designing the visuals for a financial presentation, as with other types of presentations, restrict each visual to a single important idea that can be read and absorbed quickly. In the waste conversion example, the successive visuals each reflected one major idea, even though each had quite a few figures. Avoid using sweeping visuals that cover half a dozen major points. Break them down into several visuals, each with a point or two. It is possible to leave one visual on the screen and talk through half a dozen points—but this gives the presentation a static feeling. The use of several successive visuals instead of one not only enables the group to absorb the information better, but also gives the presentation a dynamic sense of movement.

Overhead Techniques that Help

Revelation

The revelation technique on an overhead projector is good for sorting out ideas and presenting them one at a time. With the transparency that compares sales projections for a number of months or years, for instance, cover the numbers with a piece of paper, and pull the paper down to reveal only one month at a time as the presentation progresses. This allows the audience to concentrate on each new bit of data. When the entire transparency has been exposed, the group has reached an understanding of the components of the whole picture.

On-Off Method

Another visual technique for controlling attention is the on-off switch method. With a transparency which has several bits of information on it, use a pointer or a pencil to point to the first. Read it, wait a moment, then turn off the projector while you explain the information. When ready for the second point, turn the projector on again and point to the second item. When the projector is turned off between lines of information, the audience must turn its attention to what you say rather than reading ahead.

Buildup by Overlays

A buildup is made by overlaying one transparency over another to add information to the chart on the screen. The buildup technique lends drama to the presentation while it focuses the attention of the audience. The first visual in a presentation to show the growth of profits in a 10-year period might show the figures from 10 years ago. The second might show the figures from 5 years ago, and the third, the figures from this year.

Make Each Visual Stand on Its Own

Each visual in a presentation should stand on its own and be largely self-explanatory. A good visual should have four elements.

1. *A simple caption—a word or short sentence—that clearly states what it shows.* The reason the visual is on the screen is summed up in the caption or headline. A headline such as "Advertising as a Percentage of Sales Costs," informs the audience about the displayed figures. If this were shortened to "Advertising Costs," an oral explanation would be required.

2. *A simple visualization of the relationship or key point to be brought out by the chart.* Use the simplest, least cluttered visual that will show the key point or demonstrate the relationship to be made. Take out data that do not contribute, since unnecessary data distracts. There is always a temptation to put interesting related material on a chart. When presenting a chart of advertising expenditures for six products, for example, one might be tempted to show comparative figures for previous years and also expenditures for advertising by competitors. The result would be a complex chart that would intrude on the main point of the presentation. Save the competitive information for a separate chart later in the presentation.

With either bar or line charts, keep the number of bars and lines to a minimum. The fewer used, the quicker the audience will grasp the point to be made.

In preparing a chart, test its effectiveness by asking the question, "What single impression will the group retain after seeing this?"

3. *Sufficient labels to make the chart clear.* Viewers must know what values are represented: months, days, dollars of sales, etc. Every important item or value on a visual should be labeled, but use no more labels than necessary. Extra labels only distract the viewers by giving them more to read; too few labels make it difficult to make sense of the chart. The type size of all labels or identifications must be large enough to be seen from any point in the room.

4. *A feeling of variety to heighten interest.* Financial presentations often need some variety to lighten them up. The use of color is a big help. Beyond that, vary the chart design. Use some charts on a white background, some on deeply colored backgrounds with the lines in contrasting colors.

Summary

In today's fast-paced business world, the role of the financial officer has changed and enlarged. Financial reporting now has a much more active role in the management conference room. The financial officer must be a communicator, able to breathe life into numbers so they tell a story with meaning.

The Financial Presentation

Should be given in language the group can understand.
Should pinpoint the specific information the group needs.

Guidelines for a Good Financial Report

- Determine precisely what this group wants to know.
- Prepare a presentation that offers only what is needed, with no extraneous information.
- Prepare visuals which emphasize the highlights. Don't project whole sheets of computer printout.
- Round off figures to simplify the presentation.
- Use normal business language, with a minimum of accounting terminology.
- Point out trends or aberrations from the norm to provide an early warning of trouble to come and give managers an opportunity to take corrective action.

Guidelines for a Good Visual

It should have:

1. The ability to stand on its own and be largely self-explanatory.
2. A simple caption that tells what it shows.
3. A simple visualization of the relationship it demonstrates.
4. Sufficient identifications or labels to make the chart clear.
5. Color to heighten interest.

15

Multilingual Meetings

Good communication at meetings can be difficult even in one's own language, as we have noted. That being the case, what happens in a meeting between people who speak different languages?

Today, business is done on a global basis. Meetings often include persons from two or more countries. Businesses have offices in other countries, and business people frequently meet with company personnel from other countries. Even smaller companies, without overseas offices, conduct business through foreign representatives. Outside the company, meetings with foreign government people on matters such as shipping and customs, reciprocal trade, etc., are routine.

Some of these meetings are simply of the "get acquainted" or "give them the company tour" type—pleasant excursions designed to make everyone feel good, where smiles and handshakes are a substitute for language communication. But more and more are serious working meetings called to solve hard business problems, make decisions, and pass information. Meetings between persons from several countries are now similar to the meetings held every day in a typical office—except for the language problem.

How does one communicate in a meeting like this?

Two Kinds of Meetings

To begin with, there are two kinds of meetings in which language problems can occur. The first is the meeting which involves bilingual people. The second involves people who don't speak—or just barely speak—the same language. Each has its own kind of problems. There are ways to solve these problems and make the road smoother. Some involve the language itself; others involve the way meeting visuals are made and presented.

Bilingual Meetings

Your company, based in the United States, has offices in Athens, Rome, Paris, Bonn, Tokyo, and London. These offices are staffed in large part by nationals of the countries in which they are located. These people usually are bilingual—they speak their own language and English as a second language. In many countries, English is taught as a required subject in schools, and the graduate entering business has some fluency in it. Managers in a company tend to think that when nearly everyone in the company is bilingual, the language problem is solved. They plan meetings with overseas personnel as if the meeting were a standard home office affair.

The method seems to work—up to a point. Thousands of "successful" meetings of this type are held every year. But those who regularly attend these meetings recognize that there are subtle problems. The meetings take longer. There is much more follow-up work, usually involving explanation and clarification of points made in the meeting. The number of memos required to round out the meeting are doubled. Often, only a part of the presentation is understood, and those attending don't complete their assignments—not because they don't want to, but because they didn't fully understand them.

The basic problem, of course, is that those attending the meeting hear the presentations in their "second" language. They are like the right-handed batter who steps to the plate a couple of times a season to bat left-handed. They are not really practiced in it. While they may be fluent enough to carry on a light conversation or find their way through airline ticket offices and customs, they are limited to a degree that we sometimes don't fully consider.

They have relatively small vocabularies—usually one meaning for each word they know. They lack practice in the use of the daily idiom, and since in English and every other language, people speak in idioms, this is a roadblock to complete understanding. Finally, they absorb word meanings in the second language at a slower rate. If the meeting speaker talks too rapidly, they may be left with only half the communication.

At a pharmaceutical meeting in Japan, a colorful speaker delivered a presentation in English to an audience made up of members of the company from various Far Eastern countries. Every member of the group spoke English, some better than others. The speaker closed by saying, "I have one more slide to show you, and then we can all go catch a snooze. We'll meet here again at 4 o'clock."

As the group filed out of the meeting room, one of the Far Easterners approached an American member of the group putting on the meeting.

"This snooze," he said. "Where do we catch it?" He pointed to his agenda. "It doesn't say."

The story is funny, but it happens every day in one form or another. Often, the misunderstood words are business terms important to the meeting yet expressed in idiomatic form. Speakers, trying to keep a meeting light and interesting, resort to the vernacular and to idiomatic expressions without realizing that they have just stepped outside the language range of some if not all of the meeting group. Frequently, the visitors are too polite or too shy to ask for an explanation. Or they take pride in their ability with the second language, no matter how limited, and don't want to admit a failure to understand it. The result is a gap in the information they take with them from the meeting.

Simplicity of Language

The solution seems obvious: Limit the language of presentations to basic words that all attendees are likely to know. Some may have a wider vocabulary range than others, but the objective of the meeting is to communicate with *everyone* in the room. Address the lowest common denominator.

Technical terminology usually is not a problem. The people in a business quickly learn the technical terms associated with it, regardless of their language background. The problem most often is in basic expressions, idiomatic expressions, or attempts by the speaker to find a different or unusual word to express a common idea. We usually try to avoid cliches, but a meeting like this may be the one place where cliche phrases are welcome. One thing about a cliche: it may be a tired expression, but at least everyone understands what it means.

At 3M, we are familiar with adhesives and the concept of adhesion, but we also are aware of the number of common or idiomatic expressions associated with the concept that can cause trouble. There is a basic vocabulary that is well understood in this field, and we have learned to stay within it for both technical and nontechnical presentations. For example, an adhesive can be a glue, a cement, a gum, an adhesive, a mucilage, a paste, and probably a lot of other things. When something adheres, it can stick, cling, cleave, hold, be fastened with, united to, attached to, joined, be glued to, etc. A person in a meeting with a limited knowledge of English may be familiar with *cement* through association with the phrase "cement highways." This person could have real trouble when a presenter talks about cementing one thing to another. Cement, to this listener, doesn't mean an adhesive. It means a hard substance used to pave highways. While he or she is trying to decipher what the presenter meant, the presentation goes forward without him or her.

There is no such thing, of course, as a cement highway. Highways are made of concrete. But people regularly use "cement highways" as an idiom and those working in a second language may have learned it that way.

A second solution is to explain immediately any word that may be misunderstood. If for some reason, *cement* is the word that must be used, it should be followed by a sentence or two of explanation that incorporate other similar words. "We now cement this sheet . . . we glue it, make it stick . . . to that sheet." With this explanation, the presenter can associate the idea with the probable vocabulary of the listeners and help them gain the needed understanding.

Techniques for Multilingual Meetings

The visuals in any presentation where language might be a problem are important and may, in fact, be the best help in solving the problem. At 3M, we have developed two techniques that help to communicate with groups consisting of people who do not really understand the language. The first is called, "speaking in outlines"; the second, "speaking in two languages."

Speaking in Outlines

In any multilingual meeting, one barrier is speed of understanding. Some members of the group are sure to find the pace of the language too fast and lose track of the subject as the presentation speeds along. What is needed is a way to give these people the chance to recover when they get behind the presenter. This is the function of the "speaking in outlines" technique.

The first step is to prepare a detailed outline of the presentation. This should consist of a main subject outline covering the entire presentation and suboutlines showing the details to be covered within the main subject. One visual showing the main subject outline is made, and then suboutline visuals are prepared—as many as necessary, with no more than six categories on each. The visuals should be clearly labeled as "Outline" and "Suboutline." Each point should appear in the outline in the same sequence in which it will be discussed.

Two overhead projectors are used for this type of presentation. The main topic outline is projected on one screen and briefly reviewed, with the presenter pointing to each topic on the visual as it is mentioned.

We customarily put a screen on each side of the podium. We open by projecting the major outline on the screen at the right. After the review, the transparency is moved to the other projector and put on the left screen, where it stays for the rest of the presentation. Now the first suboutline visual is put up on the right screen. The presenter circles the first topic on the major outline with a felt marker, then moves back to discuss the details of it shown on the suboutline. When that subject is finished, the presenter circles the second topic on the main outline and projects the second suboutline visual. In this manner, everyone in the group not only knows exactly where the presentation is at any moment, but can, if necessary, review what has gone before it to catch up.

Charts or other visuals in the presentation are projected on the suboutline screen at the proper time. The suboutline is taken down for this, then put back up again when the charts have been discussed (Figure 15.1). We have found that almost any audience with minimal facility in the language of the presentation can follow the subject matter through this technique. It doesn't guarantee that every member of the group will grasp every point, but we know it will measurably improve the total communication.

Speaking in Two Languages

Assume that you must plan an important meeting on international marketing strategy for the coming year. Most of the overseas group you meet with speak fluent French and varying degrees of English, from poor to moderately well. Your group speaks fluent English and little French. Neither language will communicate surely to the whole group, but because of the importance of the meeting, there is no room for poor communication. You must have a presentation technique that will communicate without fail. The most obvious way would be to make a dual presentation, one in French and one in English, but that would be clumsy and would eliminate the needed interaction. We have found that a further development of the "speaking in outlines" technique, which we call "speaking in two languages," works. It does, however, require the use of an interpreter.

In this technique, the same type of major topic and subtopic visual outlines used in the "speaking in outlines" method are developed, but in the language of the majority of the meeting group—in this case, French. The presenter speaks English so the English version of the outline is written on the frame of the visual, where it can be read easily by the presenter.

The talk is delivered in English. Using the notes on the frame of the visual (Figure 15.2), the presenter is able to point to each topic, shown in French on the screen, as it is addressed. Simultaneously, an interpreter translates the presenter's talk. In this method, the presenter, with the aid of the visuals and the interpreter, speaks in both languages of the audience—English and French.

When developing this type of presentation, work carefully with the interpreter, who should be given the meeting script in advance. If there is no formal script, an elaborate set of speaker's notes should be available. It is important to have a run-through if not a full rehearsal prior to the meeting, so the presenter and the interpreter can learn to work comfortably together. This method is extremely effective as a communications device. It is somewhat more expensive than other meetings—but is economically sound because it avoids a lot of later duplicated communication. In our experience, this is the surest and

OUTLINE

**TRAINING FOR
SERVICE PERSONNEL**

I. ROLE OF CUSTOMER SERVICE
  TRAINING

II. ORGANIZATION OF A CUSTOMER
  SERVICE WORKSHOP

III. ANALYSIS OF SERVICE RESULTS

SUBOUTLINE

I. ROLE OF CUSTOMER
  SERVICE TRAINING

A. MINIMIZE BREAKDOWNS,
  MAXIMIZE USAGE, INCREASE
  PRODUCT SUPPLY
  CONSUMPTION.

B. INCREASE PROFIT.

C. AID CUSTOMER.

Figure 15.1

most effective way to bridge the language barrier. It works especially well where meetings last a full day or longer. Long sessions or meetings one after the other in which members of the group must fight their language deficiency hour after hour are extremely tiring.

Using an Interpreter

When you face the prospect of making a speech to a group which doesn't speak your language, and don't have the advantages of any special presentation technique to back you up, the best solution is to employ an interpreter. Until you have done it a few times, using an interpreter seems clumsy, but once you have become familiar with the routine, it is

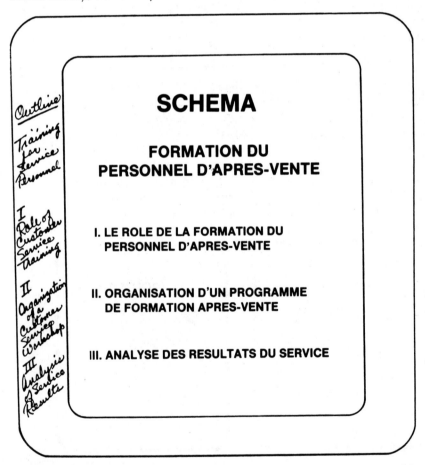

Figure 15.2

easy. The secret is close cooperation between you and the interpreter. Here are a few guidelines to follow to make even your first experience with an interpreter a pleasant one:

1. Use a script and follow it fairly closely. We don't recommend that you read from it, but rather that you deal with the subjects in the order they appear on the script without deviation. Give the interpreter a few hours to go over the speech and become familiar with your style and phrasing, and with the general subject matter. The two of you should discuss any technical terms with which the interpreter is not familiar. If you intend to use charts or other visuals, show the interpreter how you will talk your way through each. Explain the point each visual is to make.

2. When speaking, remember that you are talking to the audience, not to the interpreter. There is always a strong temptation to look at and address the interpreter, but it should be resisted. Face the audience and keep facing them as the interpreter speaks. Keep your voice at the normal speaking level. Don't lower it to the conversational level, as you might when speaking to the interpreter.

3. An interpreter has a tricky job. He or she must hear your words, remember them, quickly translate or paraphrase them, and then speak them accurately. To facilitate this process, break your talk into easily managed bites. Deliver several sentences or a paragraph, then wait for the interpreter to translate. If you say too much, the interpreter will try to catch the sense of what you said, but will probably be forced to condense and perhaps skip some. Discuss this timing with the interpreter beforehand.

4. Keep the presentation unified for the listener by speaking about only one idea or full thought at a time. This gives the interpreter a better chance to be accurate in the translation.

5. Remember that the use of an interpreter doubles the time of the meeting. Allow for the expanded time on the meeting agenda.

Where to Find an Interpreter

One way to find an interpreter is through the language department of the nearest college or university. Staff members or graduate students often are available for a nominal fee. The department head also knows of professional interpreters in the area and usually will make recommendations.

Many times, you must be concerned not only with the presentation but also with printed materials to accompany it. It is a good idea to have at least some of the printed pieces—the agenda, for example, and directions to meeting rooms, details about accommodations, etc.—in the language of the attendees. Translators for the material can be found through the college or university language department.

Your own employees, especially in a big corporation with a large people base to draw from, are one resource that should be tapped in solving language problems. It is not unusual to find a number of bilingual employees in departments that would seldom if ever be involved in a multilingual presentation. Many times, they come from families where another language is or has been spoken. In other cases, they had language training in school. Compile a list of these people and screen them for both ability and availability. You may be able to assemble an internal language "consultants" group this way.

Learning a Language Yourself

This chapter has been addressed mainly to English-speaking business people who have no facility in any other language. As business has broadened through the world, language barriers have broken down. More and more business people have at least a passing ability in a second language and often that language is English. Americans, however, are notorious for not learning other languages while all over the world others are learning English.

We recommend to anyone involved in multilingual presentations that they learn another language. The chief value, at least in the beginning, is not that presentations can be given in the new language—but that one develops a strong appreciation for the difficulties of multilingual communication. When struggling to learn conversational Spanish or French or German, you find out how difficult it is to listen to someone who speaks too rapidly or who uses uncommon words. This knowledge forces you to make better presentations before multilingual audiences.

The Customs of Other Countries

Joe Ramos, Area Vice President for Latin America, has served as Managing Director of 3M Divisions in other countries. He says, "When attending or conducting meetings in other countries, you must be sensitive to cultural differences. Meetings go more smoothly when the national customs of all those in the room are taken into account."

Persons engaged in global business have learned to be tolerant of those who don't observe their customs, but the general atmosphere improves when visitors recognize thoughtful touches by those sponsoring the meeting. These range from small items such as serving tea as well as coffee during breaks—the kind of tea preferred by your guests—to the rigorous observation of formalities. Americans tend to become informal very quickly, getting on a first-name basis in a short time. We also have tendencies to touch others—hold an arm, slap a back, poke a finger. People of other countries usually prefer to remain on a pleasant, very polite but formal basis. For the most part, they dislike touching and talk that is too familiar. They usually are very sensitive about titles; introductions should always include the full titles of those you are introducing.

Almost every country has certain customs in regard to food and drink. Alcoholic beverages are accepted as a part of entertainment in many countries, but may be out of place in meetings with persons from others. Visitors enjoy sampling American food, as a rule, rather than food in their own cuisine, but the menu should not feature items they cannot eat for religious or other reasons.

If your company has overseas offices, observance of customs should not be a problem. Foreign nationals on your staff have learned to adapt to the company's manners, and your people have learned how to observe their customs. If, however, you plan to meet with a group you don't know, do a little homework. A telephone call to the nearest consulate can produce a quick list of things to do and not to do.

Summary

Language problems occur in two kinds of meetings:

1. The meeting which involves bilingual people.
BASIC PROBLEM: The group hears the presentations in its second language, in which they may have limited vocabularies and lack practice in the use of the idiom.
THE SOLUTION: Limit the language of presentations to basic words that all attendees are likely to know.
SECOND PROBLEM: Group finds the pace of the language too fast and gets lost as the presentation proceeds.
SOLUTION: Keep the pace of the delivery slow enough to be understood.

2. The meeting with people who don't speak—or just barely speak—the language.
BASIC PROBLEM: Communication in your language simply won't work.

SOLUTION: Use a presentation involving both languages. Two techniques can help in communicating with people who do not understand the language.

Speak in Outlines

1. Prepare visuals showing an outline of the main subject and suboutlines with details to be covered within the main subject. Visuals should be labeled "Outline" and "Suboutline."

2. Use two overhead projectors. Project main topic outline on one screen and briefly review it, pointing to each topic on the visual as it is mentioned.

3. After the review, move the transparency to the other projector, leaving it on the screen for the remainder of the session.

4. Project first suboutline visual. Use a marker to circle the first topic on the major outline, then move back to discuss details as shown on the suboutline.

5. When that subject is finished, circle the second topic on the main outline and put up the second suboutline visual.

6. Charts or other visuals are projected on the suboutline screen at the proper time. The suboutline is put back up again when the charts have been discussed.

Any audience with minimal language facility can follow the subject matter through this technique and can review and catch up whenever necessary.

Speak in Two Languages

This technique requires the use of an interpreter. Major topic and subtopic visual outlines also are used, but they are in the language of the majority of the meeting group.

1. The presenter delivers the talk in his or her own language. Observing notes on the frame of the visual, the presenter points to each topic as it is addressed.

2. An interpreter simultaneously translates the presenter's talk.

3. The projection of visuals is handled as in the "speaking in outlines" technique.

In effect, the presenter, with the aid of the visuals and the interpreter, speaks in both languages of the audience.

16

Staff and Committee Meetings

"It's a pleasure to attend a good staff meeting," an executive told us. "You leave with a feeling that you've observed teamwork in action."

The staff meeting is the primary working tool of every organizational group within a company, from small departments to divisions and groups right up to top management. The staff meeting has been aptly described as the glue which holds any working group together and also as one means by which any staff can get its unity recharged.

A staff meeting can be used for communication, work review, problem solving, planning, brainstorming, and a dozen other reasons. Very often a single staff meeting embodies half a dozen of these items. Compared to the agenda of a standard business meeting such as we have described earlier, which tends to deal with one subject, the staff meeting menu of activity often is a real pot pourri. The variety of these agendas helps to keep them interesting, but at the same time, often lends them a feeling of disorientation.

The major weakness of many staff meetings is that they are too often routine—called just because it's Monday, which may be the worst reason in the world to call a meeting. Too often, out-of-touch managers use them to catch up with what's going on in the department when they should have known all about it last week. Staff meetings tie up the whole staff for an hour or more, bring departmental work to a standstill, and are costly in workhours.

On the other hand, staff meetings are valuable because they keep staff members informed about what's going on in the department and alert to new projects. They are most valuable if scheduled when needed, and not just because it's Monday. They also need to be tightly organized, and run from a good agenda even if the agenda covers half an acre of topics.

The automatically scheduled weekly staff meeting tends not to have an agenda. Each member of the group arrives with some ideas that need discussion and brings them up at the first opportunity. These meetings often open with the uninspiring statement from the meeting leader, "Well, what do we have to talk about today?" From this point forward, discussion is unstructured and allowed to take any direction.

Formula for Effective Staff Meetings

The main objectives of a staff meeting are to transmit or clarify ideas, problems, or decisions; to get participation in problem solving; to motivate staff; and to help employees act as a cohesive group. They are a powerful two-way communications tool when used properly. They should be held as often as necessary—but only when necessary. If the manager feels that regularly scheduled staff meetings work for his or her group, we suggest that the regular meetings be limited to one a month, and that other meetings be held in between as need dictates.

The meeting should have an agenda to guide the discussion. An automatic agenda can be useful when one cannot be specially prepared. An automatic agenda might include:

1. Work review. Reports on departmental activity and assignments by each group member.
2. Presentations of problems and discussion of solutions.
3. Planning, discussion of new activity, new work assignments.
4. New idea and suggestion forum.

This agenda serves at least to compartmentalize the meeting and keep discussion on an orderly track. Knowing that a format such as this is always followed provides some guidance for staff members in getting ready for the meeting.

Employees' View of Staff Meetings

The most common complaints we hear about staff meetings are that they're too routine, too infrequent, and not well run. An equally common complaint is that they are held too often. This diversity of opinion makes it difficult to know exactly what people think is wrong with staff meetings.

Our observation is that employees consider staff meetings to have a very high personal value. They see their own business lives more affected by staff meetings than others. They feel that their progress in the organization is more likely to depend on activity in staff meetings. As a rule, they want involvement and participation, but they fear that they may suffer from being too outspoken. They hope through staff meetings to understand their role in the organization. They want information that will give them clues as to where they are going. They want to know how their activities fit into the larger scope of their supervisor's plans and actions. They look to staff meetings to provide this kind of information.

For this reason perhaps as much as any other, staff meetings are important. They represent an important point of company contact for each group member and out of this contact grows motivation—or lack of it—and personal commitment to the job. It is possible that staff meetings are much criticized because many of these meetings don't fulfill the personal needs of group members.

The manager needs to be sensitive to this personal side of staff meetings. This means providing ample opportunity for each person to speak freely and without fear of criticism or reprisal; listening patiently to discussion that may be off the mark; holding back criticisms and delivering them later in private meetings with staff members; passing along helpful, insightful information on the company and its policies to provide the staff with a feeling of being "on the inside." Throughout the meeting, there should be a current of encouragement to motivate the staff people. New ideas, in particular, should be encouraged.

The climate of a staff meeting should be congenial, expressive, and constructive in order to nourish good communication. To a large degree, this climate is set by the manager. Perhaps the manager's most important, and sometimes most difficult, job at a staff meeting is to listen. With a head full of departmental problems, managers may find listening painful at times. But not listening is tantamount to admitting he or she really doesn't care to learn what's on the minds of the staff. When that happens, motivation suffers.

Committee Meetings

There is a common belief that when any proposal in business or politics is referred to a committee, its obituary has just been written. This belief, true or not, demonstrates the poor reputation of committees as "graveyards of progress."

Committees are neither all bad nor all good. Some companies are organized around the committee system and make very effective use of the form. In general, though, the committee is a form of organization that cuts across the normal lines of command. It usually is given responsibility for a specific mission. Committees are sometimes created for the mission and disbanded when their work is accomplished. At other times, they are given permanent or semipermanent lives to work on ongoing projects.

Committees are called for fact-finding, planning, review, and other complex tasks that cannot be done through the existing organization. Their effectiveness depends almost entirely on the ability of the chair to organize the task, parcel out the work, and run tightly controlled meetings as the work progresses. A poorly run committee is worse than no committee at all.

Almost equally important as the chair is the committee's secretary—the second in command or executive officer of the group. Much of the day-to-day work behind the scenes falls on the secretary, who must be able to work smoothly with the chairperson. The secretary has the interesting problem of working hard without in any way assuming the leadership of the committee—or of permitting others to think that he or she has control.

Before a committee is formed, its assigned mission should be defined because the mission is a strong factor in the selection of the chair, secretary, and committee personnel.

How Many People on a Committee?

Committees have been known to founder because of size alone. All too often, appointment to a committee is done as a means of recognizing (in business) or honoring (in public life) someone. It is important when establishing a committee to keep in mind that the group has real work to do. Deadwood on a committee is no better than deadwood in a regular business meeting.

In general, it can be assumed that the larger the committee, the longer it will take for the work of the group to be completed. In most cases, the committee operates in either a task force or review capacity. In a review committee, the number of members is not as critical; in a task force, the number of members can seriously affect the group's work.

Task Force Committee

The work of a task force committee proceeds through a series of well-defined steps. Assume that a company plans to celebrate 100 years in business next year. A committee is formed to make plans for the celebration. The first phase of the work is to explore all possible avenues of the celebration—banquets, advertising, awards, memorial grants, a company picnic, anniversary sales events, etc. When a list has been drawn up, each member of the committee is assigned to research tasks and asked to report back on costs and feasibility of items on the list.

When the reports are in, the committee reviews all possibilities and draws up a plan incorporating those items which seem best based on cost and effectiveness. The plan is refined, priced out, and individual events are given dates, and the committee then draws up its anniversary plan and submits it to management.

All task force work follows the same general pattern, whether the committee has been asked to investigate salary levels in the industry or plan an event. Whatever its task, the committee's effectiveness depends on the chair's ability to generate discussion and, as a result of it, assign work, and on the willingness of the members to carry out the tasks assigned to them. Most committees bog down in one or the other of these areas. It can be seen, then, that committee members must be prepared to work along with the chair if the work is to be completed on a timely basis.

Review Committee

A review committee operates much like a court of law. It sits, listens, and then makes a determination. There may be work assignments to members in some instances—as when the task is to review a change in employee hospitalization plans. The committee must research the possible options, which may require individual work assignments, and then make a recommendation to management. Typical assignments for a review committee might include reviews of company policies, disciplinary actions, wage and salary scales, health and benefit plans, new construction, etc.

Designing the Successful Committee

The design of a committee is at least in part determined by the work assigned to the group. Guidelines for the establishment of a committee would include:

1. Select a self-starting chair, preferably someone qualified in the subject with which the committee must deal.
2. Select an energetic secretary to carry out the work of the chair. Think of the secretary as someone qualified to be a project manager.
3. Select group members qualified to serve by their knowledge and ability to devote sufficient time to the project. The number should be limited by such considerations as meeting facilities, amount of research to be performed, etc. Keep the committee as small as practical to facilitate discussion.
4. Define the task of the committee in concrete terms. The success of the group may depend on how well their objective is defined for them.
5. Suggest that the committee set regular meeting dates and observe them scrupulously. The committee which meets occasionally "when necessary" falls apart easily and gets little done.
6. Set time limits on the term of the committee or on when the work must be finished. Most groups work better with a deadline in view.
7. If the committee is permanent and its work ongoing, establish terms of tenure and a plan for rotation of personnel. This brings fresh new ideas to the group on a regular schedule.
8. Make it clear that interim progress reports are expected on a regular basis.

Meetings below Management Level

This book is addressed to executives and managers, but in recent years, the meeting has taken on a new and critical dimension. Thanks at least in part to Japanese manufacturing companies, it has been learned that communication below the management level can cut production costs and increase quality. Many companies are now calling or permitting meetings of plant and production personnel—the so-called "Quality Circle" meetings. Good ideas and creative participation in the company's business, it has been discovered, are not limited to the upper echelon.

Meetings of people below the management level introduce a new problem. Here we have eager, interested, involved people who want to communicate but haven't had the daily meeting experience of management personnel. Specific techniques to help these meetings need to be developed.

The meeting techniques covered in this book apply in general to these meetings as well as to those at management level. While a meeting in the plant may not have the polish of the meeting in the board rooms, the basic need for good communication is just as important.

Plant meetings need good leadership. Some are run by management personnel, while others are run by plant personnel, sometimes with advisory help from management. No particular pattern for success has yet emerged; both kinds of meetings have succeeded. However, when the meetings are run by management personnel, there is a risk that the heavy hand of management may stifle plant employee participation. Those who attend these meetings want a strong sense of participation, of being listened to, and of making a contribution. If they sense that what they are saying isn't being heard, they back away and the meetings fail.

Meeting Leadership through Training

To encourage participation and provide the necessary meeting leadership skills, many companies have developed training seminars. Held during working hours, these usually are open to all supervisors and foremen and sometimes to all plant personnel. The objective of these seminars is not to make professional meetings leaders of those who attend, but rather to acquaint them with the fundamentals of the meeting. Items covered include:

How to lead a meeting. In the seminar, trainees are given instruction in opening a meeting, calling for ideas and discussion, disciplining recalcitrant group members, and steering a discussion through to a logical conclusion.

How to use an agenda. A part of meeting leadership is the construction and use of a meeting agenda. Training covers such things as how to manage meeting time by reference to the agenda, soliciting agenda items, etc.

Training programs can be developed from chapters in this book on these aspects of the meeting. Seminar attendees can be given "hands on" experience in the class to increase proficiency. All of those who "graduate" can be given certificates that qualify them as plant meeting leaders.

Summary

The staff meeting is the primary working tool of every organizational group within a company, from small departments to divisions and groups, right up to top management.

Formula for Effective Staff Meetings

The meeting should have an agenda to guide the discussion. An automatic agenda can be useful when one cannot be specially prepared. An automatic agenda might include:

1. Work review. Reports on departmental activity and assignments by each group member.
2. Presentations of problems and discussion of solutions.
3. Planning, discussion of new activity, new work assignments.
4. New idea and suggestion forum.

The agenda serves at least to compartmentalize the meeting and keep discussion on an orderly track. Knowing that a format such as this is always followed provides some guidance for staff members in getting ready for the meeting.

How to Design a Committee

The design of a committee is in part determined by the work assigned to the group. Guidelines include:

1. Select a self-starting chair—someone qualified in the subject with which the committee must deal.
2. Select an energetic secretary to carry out the work of the chair and serve as project manager.
3. Select group members qualified to serve by their knowledge and with sufficient time to devote to the project. Keep the committee as small as practical to facilitate discussion.
4. Define the task of the committee in concrete terms.
5. Suggest that the committee set regular meeting dates.
6. Set time limits on the term of the committee or on when the work must be finished.
7. If the committee is permanent and its work on-going, establish terms of tenure and a plan for rotation.
8. Require interim progress reports on a regular basis.

Conclusion

Excellence in management.

It isn't easy to relate daily business meetings to the concept of excellence in management. The executive or manager trudging down the hall with notes tucked under the arm, headed for the next meeting, is seldom motivated by such inspirational thoughts. But the ordinary everyday meeting is closely related to excellence in management.

Much like the mammoth jigsaw puzzle with 3000 pieces, business is complex and any given meeting represents only one tiny piece of the puzzle. If the picture, when it finally comes together, is to be perfect, then each piece in the puzzle must be perfect—because each piece contributes its share.

These days, more than in the past, businesses are being singled out for excellence and for innovative ideas. The corporate world is taking a hard look at itself and discovering the meaning of excellence. The search is on to find those things which contribute to excellence, to find out how excellence is achieved.

In making our own search, we have recognized that meetings are a critical component of business. In a way, the entire decision-making process that we call business is a series of meetings—meetings to get information, meetings to impart information, meetings to explore possibilities and capabilities, meetings to rub ideas together, meetings to marshall the facts and make decisions.

Since that is the case, it stands to reason that the quality of individual meetings contributes to the quality of the operation of the business. Weakness in meetings takes away from the quality of business operation. It comes down to the fact that one major element of excellence in business management must be the quality of the meetings on which that management depends so heavily.

To write a book that takes an in-depth look at meetings and then to present this book to the corporate world—which is immersed in daily meetings—at first seems to be truly like "carrying coal to Newcastle." But on second look, it appears that Newcastle these days is very much in need of coal. If we had not been on the firing line daily, struggling with the problems of meeting improvement, perhaps we wouldn't have seen it. But see it we did. And our conclusion was that any company in search of excellence has only two basic places to look: at the quality of its people and at the quality of the way its people communicate: in other words, the employees and how well they meet and work together.

Company attitudes and policy grow out of the people and the interplay of their opinions. Together, these things create a company atmosphere, a company character, a company outlook, and eventually, company achievement. At 3M, we have achieved a reputation for excellence. A close look at our company reveals that this reputation springs from a companywide respect for our people, their ideas, and their creativity, coupled with a very serious concern for how they work together.

This book is not the last word on meetings. It represents a look at the state of the art today. But tomorrow there will be more improvements, and we expect to continue to learn.

Index

About the Authors

The 3M Meeting Management Team is a group of six meeting management experts whose backgrounds include all facets of corporate enterprise—administration, marketing, sales, communications, training, technical, and international operations. Five are presently employed by 3M's Audio Visual Division: Stephen P. Birkeland, Ph.D., technical director; David J. Cooper, marketing operations manager; Marshall Hatfield, Ph.D., division vice president; Virginia "Gini" Johnson, market development and training manager; and Frank E. Poole, marketing director. The sixth member, Joseph M. Ramos, M.B.A., is 3M's area vice president for Latin America.

STEPHEN P. BIRKELAND

Dr. Birkeland joined 3M's Central Research Laboratories after receiving his Ph.D. from the University of New Mexico in 1959 and completing a postdoctoral fellowship at Stanford University. In 1972 he transferred to the Visual Products Division and undertook various technical management positions. Prior to accepting his current position as technical director of the Audio Visual Division, Dr. Birkeland served as the division's product control manager worldwide. He has personally accomplished a number of product development achievements, including design of 3M's Model 840 Full Color Transparency Maker. He has been granted nine U.S. patents and produced several major technical publications in the areas of imaging and photographic science.

DAVID J. COOPER

As marketing operations manager for the Audio Visual Division, Dave Cooper is responsible for the division's complete range of marketing activities. He began his career at 3M in 1965 as a sales representative. During his more than 20 years with the company he has had a number of sales management assignments including that of national sales manager. These positions of increasing responsibility have given Mr. Cooper a broad range of meeting experiences, not only at 3M, but also with other Fortune 1000 companies, as he worked to help solve their meeting management problems.

214

DR. MARSHALL HATFIELD

Dr. Marshall Hatfield joined 3M in 1950 after completing a Ph.D. in chemistry at the University of Illinois. Despite his scientific background, however, Dr. Hatfield soon found himself working in administrative positions of increasing responsibility. He became technical director of 3M's Microfilm Division, developed the company's Computer Graphics Project in 1969, and then took over the New Business Ventures Division. Following this assignment, Dr. Hatfield took over 3M's Mincom Division, which included Wollensak recording equipment. In 1981, following a companywide reorganization, Wollensak and Dr. Hatfield went to the Visual Products Division—manufacturer of 3M's highly successful overhead projection line. With the merger of the audio and visual lines, the Audio Visual Division was born. There he orchestrated the development of the division as "The How to Meeting People."

VIRGINIA "GINI" JOHNSON

More than 20 years of experience in education, personnel, learning resource development, training, and marketing have provided a broad background for Gini Johnson's interest and expertise in effective meetings. As manager of Market Development and Training for 3M's Audio Visual Division, Ms. Johnson is responsible for product marketing, sales, and customer training, telemarketing, and a National Seminar Program serving more than 100 locations. She is currently working on the development of an International Meeting Management Institute. During the past 5 years, Ms. Johnson has conducted over 200 public service programs on quality of business communications, including a series of eight national seminars sponsored by *Working Woman Magazine*. She has also authored numerous articles on meeting and presentation skills. Ms. Johnson is completing an M.S. in organizational leadership.

FRANK E. POOLE

Mr. Poole has been actively involved in the management of the Audio Visual Division for many years, serving as marketing director since 1976. He was instrumental in leading the division into the commercial market, which is the major segment of the division's business. Poole, who has a B.A. in economics from the College of St. Thomas, joined 3M in 1959. His prior positions include sales manager of the Duplicating Products Division and national sales manager for Industrial Markets. His extensive sales and marketing-related activities have led to direct involvement with all types of customers, including those of the Fortune 1000. Mr. Poole has been an active contributor to a number of the "How to" meeting publications developed by the Audio Visual Division.

JOSEPH M. RAMOS

Though only 45 years of age, Joseph Ramos has almost 30 years with 3M. Mr. Ramos joined a 3M distributor in Los Angeles for a summer sales job while in high school. He continued in a part-time capacity while completing his university studies and has been with the company in varying capacities ever since. Mr. Ramos has held positions ranging from sales representative to area vice president for Latin America. During his career he has served as 3M's managing director in both Puerto Rico and Argentina. His broad sales, administrative, and international experience give Mr. Ramos a global perspective on the business meeting and its increasingly important role in the efficient conduct of corporate affairs. Mr. Ramos has a B.A. in English from UCLA and an M.B.A. in Finance from Pepperdine University, Los Angeles.